OAKWOOD LIBRARY OF RAILWAY HIS

THE WELLS-NEXT-THE-SEA BRANCH

VIA WYMONDHAM AND DEREHAM

by
S.C. Jenkins, M.A.

THE OAKWOOD PRESS

ISBN 0 85361 374 5

Typesetting by Gem Publishing Company, Brightwell, Wallingford, Oxfordshire

Printed and Bound by Bocardo Press Ltd, Didcot.

Published by
The OAKWOOD PRESS
P.O.Box 122, Headington, Oxford.

Contents

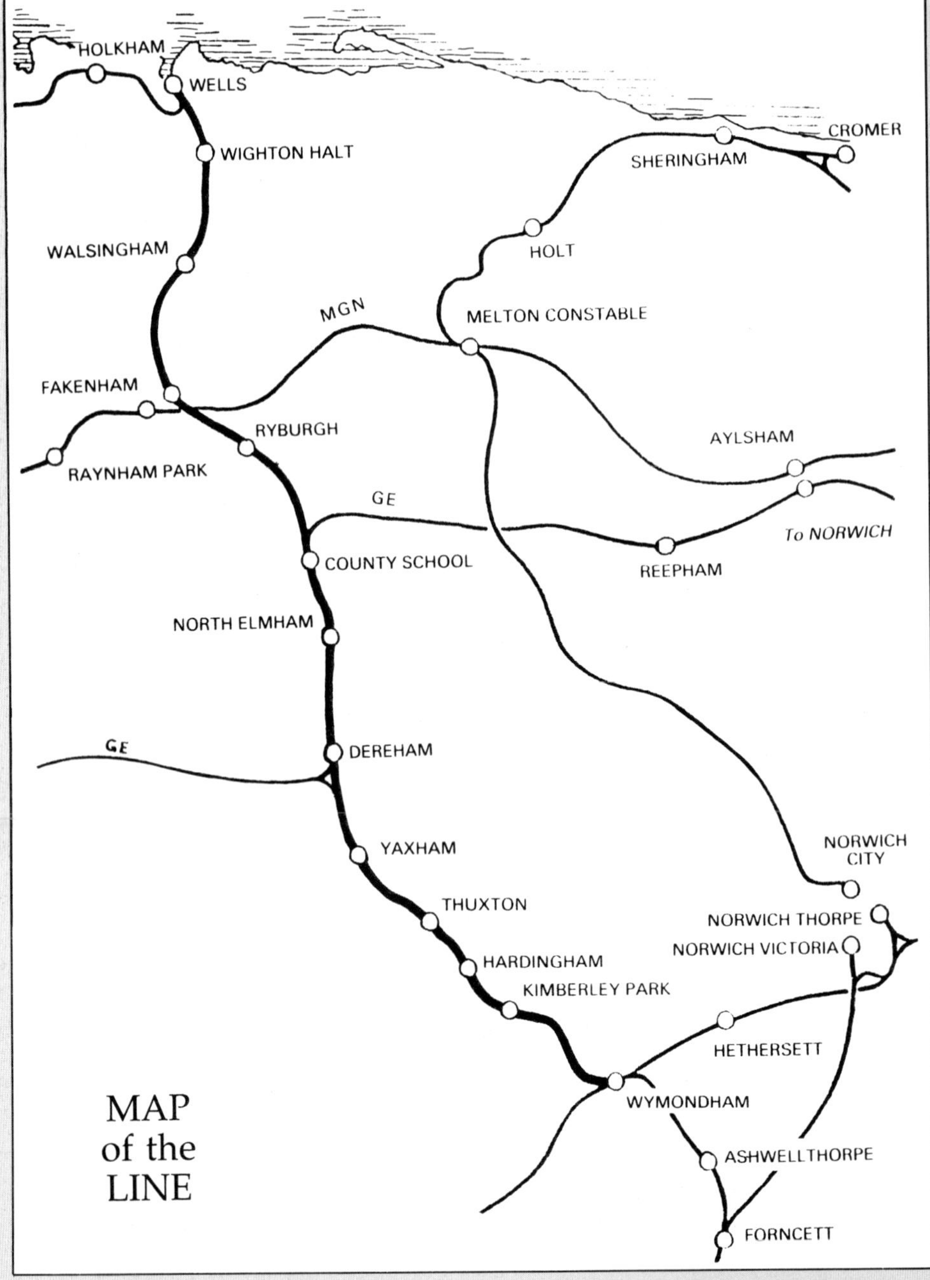

MAP
of the
LINE

Historical Summary

COMPANIES OF ORIGIN (1) THE NORFOLK RAILWAY

An amalgamation of the Yarmouth & Norwich (incorporated 18th June, 1842) and Norwich & Brandon (incorporated 1844) under an Act of 30th June, 1845; opened from Norwich to Gt Yarmouth on 1st May, 1844 and from Norwich to Brandon on 29th July, 1845, the two sections being linked on 15th December to form a continuous route from Brandon (where a connection was made with the Eastern Counties) to Gt Yarmouth. The Norfolk Railway was worked by the ECR from 8th May, 1848. Amalgamated with GER 1862.

COMPANIES OF ORIGIN (2) THE WELLS & FAKENHAM RAILWAY

Incorporated 24th July, 1854 (17 & 18 Vic. cap 180) with capital of £70,000 in £20 shares and borrowing powers of £23,000. On 13th August, 1859 the company was empowered to extend its line along Wells quay, and raise additional capital of £3,800 at 6% preference with loan of £1,200 to convert debenture debt into stock; by the same Act the Norfolk Railway was empowered to guarantee interest on the new capital of £3,800, providing that annual revenue would so permit. Working agreements with Norfolk and ECR never satisfactorily resolved. Amalgamated with GER 1862.

WELLS & FAKENHAM DIRECTORS (1857)

Chairman – Sir Samuel Morton Peto, Bart., Somerleyton Hall, Suffolk

Richard Till (Norfolk Railway Chairman)
Horatio Bolingbroke, Norwich
Jacob Watson of 59 Burton Crescent, London
Hall William Keary, Holkham
Joseph Springhill Southgate, Wells

Secretary, Mr Hutt; Engineer, George Berkeley

Dates of Opening

Wymondham to Dereham (Norfolk), 7th December, 1846 (Goods)
15th February, 1847 (Passenger)
Dereham to Fakenham (Norfolk), 20th March, 1849
Fakenham to Wells (W&FR), 1st December, 1857

Length of Branch

(Wymondham-Wells),	33 miles 3 chains
(Norwich Thorpe-Wells),	43 miles 21 chains

Mode of Operation

Double line block between Wymondham and Dereham North Box; Tyer's No. 6 Tablet between Dereham North Box and North Elmham; Train Staff & Ticket system between North Elmham and Wells.

Crossing Loops on Single Line

North Elmham, County School, Fakenham (Walsingham was a staff station but had no loop, and Ryburgh had a loop but was not a staff station).

Typical Motive Power

'E4' 2–4–0s, 'J15' 0–6–0s, 'D13' 4–4–0s, 'D15' 4–4–0s, 'D16/2/3' 4–4–0s, 'F3' 2–4–2Ts, 'J17' 0–6–0s.

Dates of Closure

Dereham–Wells, Saturday 3rd October, 1964 (Passenger), remaining open for goods until 31st October, 1964.

Wymondham–Dereham, Saturday 4th October, 1969 (Passenger).

Date of Re-opening

Wells to Walsingham as 10¼ inch gauge line on 6th April, 1982.

Introduction

Running for 33 miles through remote, yet surprisingly attractive Norfolk countryside, the branch line from Wymondham to Wells-next-the-Sea was one of the most picturesque routes in East Anglia. The line was opened in stages and had two distinct parts; its southernmost section (from Wymondham to Dereham) was opened in 1846 and became part of a cross country route to Kings Lynn just two years later. The line was extended to Fakenham in 1849 and completed throughout to Wells-next-the-Sea in 1857; the section from Wymondham to Fakenham was part of the Norfolk Railway, but the northernmost extremity of the route belonged to the Wells & Fakenham Railway – a small, locally-based company. The Wells-next-the-Sea branch was from its inception worked by the Eastern Counties Railway, though it never came under full ECR control, and the owning companies retained their independence until both became part of the Great Eastern Railway in 1862.

The line ran to the seaside, but it never developed as a true "seaside branch" because Wells only became a tourist centre in the 1950s and 1960s. It remained a rural branch line, serving local agricultural industries – indeed, much of the route remains *in situ* as part of the

BR network, albeit as a freight-only branch rather than as a passenger line. However, the northern end of the route has found a new and novel use as a narrow gauge tourist line, and the Wells & Walsingham Railway – the world's longest 10¼ in. gauge line – now occupies much of the former trackbed.

Although the former Great Eastern branch lines in East Anglia were, collectively, some of the most interesting branches in Britain, they have not hitherto enjoyed much attention from writers and historians, and the present history is the first monograph to appear in print on the Wells-next-the-Sea branch. The opening of the Wells & Walsingham Railway has focused popular attention on the northern part of the line, and for this reason the narrative concentrates primarily (though not exclusively) on the former Wells & Fakenham section. Nevertheless, branch train services operated on a Wells –Fakenham–Dereham–Norwich axis, and it is impossible to tell the story of the Wells & Fakenham in isolation; thus, in this present study, the "Wells branch" has been defined as a dead end branch, diverging from the main line at Wymondham – a distance of 33 miles.

Stanley C. Jenkins
Witney, Oxfordshire

A Note on Place Names

The correct name of Wells is Wells-next-the-Sea, this being a translation from the Latin Wells-*juxta-Mare*; however, the LNER called the station Wells-on-Sea, and this name remained in use until BR changed the name to Wells-next-the-Sea in 1957. (When first opened in 1857 the station was called simply "Wells"). North Elmham was originally called "Elmham", and Kimberley Park was, until 1923, known as "Kimberley".

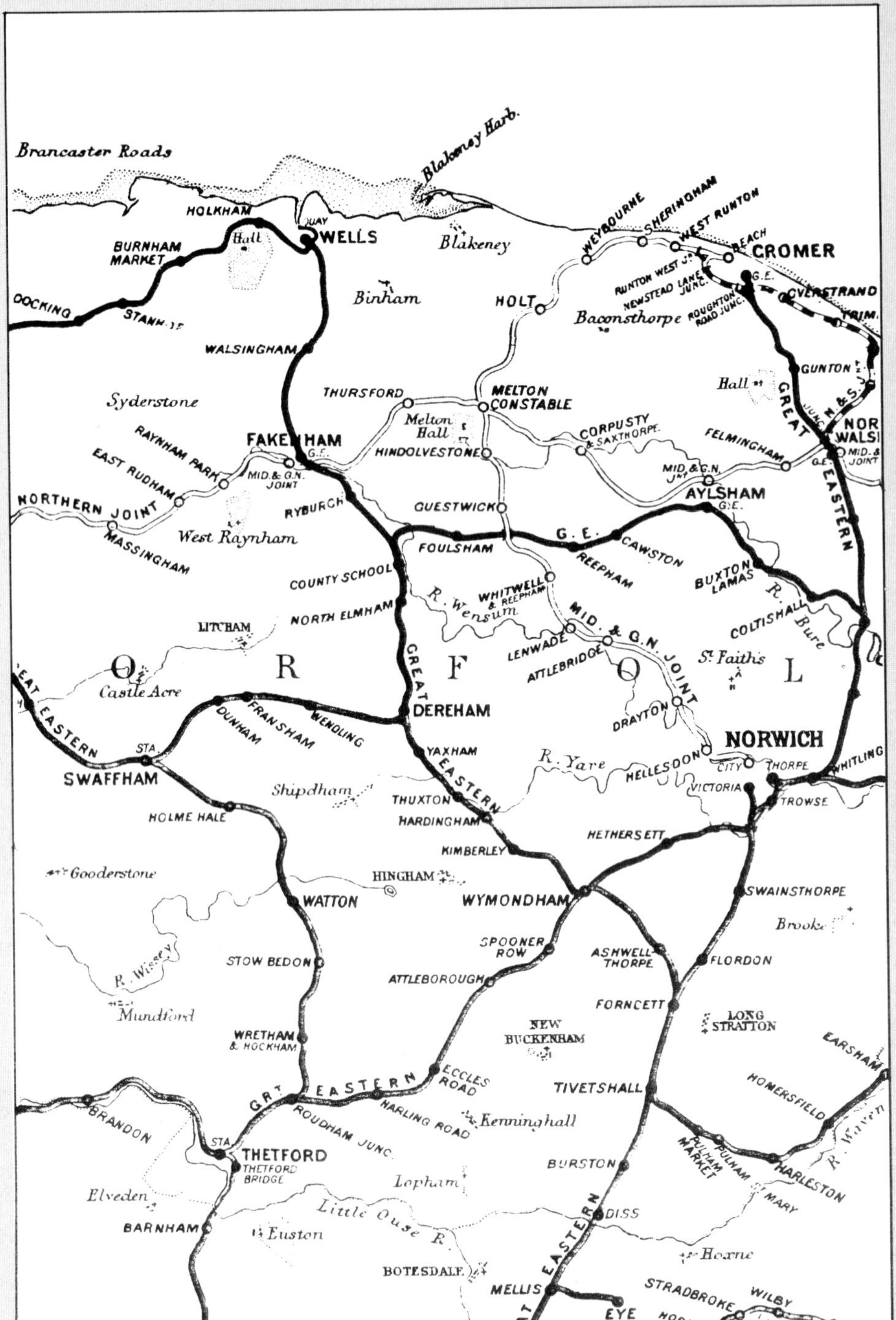

The Railway Clearing House map, *c.*1910.

Chapter One

Origins, Opening and Early Years (1840–1857)

Wells-next-the-Sea is a small town and seaport, situated on the remote, northern coast of Norfolk, approximately 35 miles to the north west of Norwich. Recorded in the Domesday Book as "Quella", Wells may have developed as a haven for nearby Warham after other local creeks had silted up. Although fishing was obviously an important activity, the little town was primarily a trading port, becoming in later years something of a ship-building centre. Imports, in the Medieval period, probably included lead and building stone destined for use at Binham Priory or Walsingham Abbey, while fish, timber and barley must have formed a considerable proportion of Wells' export trade. By the end of the Middle Ages, "Wells-juxta-Mare" had emerged as a place of considerable importance, with ship yards, rope walks, wharves, several inns and no less than three churches.

In earlier times, Wells "town centre" was situated in the vicinity of St Nicholas's Church, with wharves and other facilities clustered around the original harbour creek. Silting (and possibly a desire to accommodate larger vessels) led to the creation of a new complex of quays and warehouses on a fresh site about half a mile to the north, and by the 17th Century most of the port facilities were concentrated along this new quay; inevitably, the "town centre" also moved northwards, with the result that Staithe Street became the town's main thoroughfare, leaving the old High Street to become a residential area.

Unlike most other sea ports, Wells was dominated by a succession of powerful local landlords and the inhabitants of the little town obviously had to respect the wishes of those who lived in "the big house" – in this case Holkham Hall, the home of the Cokes. Fortunately, the Cokes were benevolent and improving landlords and, far from retarding development, they actively encouraged it. In 1776 the Holkham estate passed to Thomas Coke (1752–1842), the celebrated "Coke of Norfolk", who (by the careful application of scientific principles) transformed his barren, sandy estate into an agricultural show-place. Adored by all classes, he was in the vanguard of an agrarian revolution that made British farming the most efficient in the world. When he first came to North Norfolk, it was said that the land was so poor that "two rabbits could be seen fighting for a single blade of grass". At that time Holkham rentals averaged just £2,200 a year, yet in a few short years Coke managed to raise this meagre figure to a staggering £20,000!

The Railways Come to Norfolk

Although in many ways a somewhat remote region, East Anglia

had never been a backward area; on the contrary, the efforts of Coke of Norfolk, Turnip Townsend and other agricultural improvers ensured that the Eastern Counties were frequently in advance of other areas. Since the Reformation, East Anglia had been a staunchly Protestant region with a long tradition of thrift, hard work and self-discipline – and East Anglians had (not surprisingly) achieved prominence in many walks of life.

Inevitably, with the rapid development of railways in other parts of the country, local traders, bankers and landowners were eager to share in the advantages of this new and revolutionary form of transport, and as early as the 1820s there were schemes designed to connect Norwich or Cambridge to London. In 1821, for example, the pioneer railway promoter William James (1771–1837) had surveyed a possible "engine railroad from Bishops Stortford to Clayhithe Sluice with a branch to Waddon", while in 1824–5 an equally-grandiose "Norfolk, Suffolk & Essex Railroad" was projected. If successful, this last-named scheme would have linked London, Norwich and Great Yarmouth, providing a viable nucleus for any future East Anglian system. These 1820s projects were hopelessly premature, and both failed to get off the ground. Nevertheless, tangible progress was made in the following decade, and on 4th July, 1836 two important schemes – the Eastern Counties Railway and the Northern & Eastern Railway – received the Royal Assent.

The Eastern Counties Railway was in effect a revival of the earlier Norfolk, Suffolk & Essex scheme, and like its abortive predecessor, the company hoped to link London with Norwich and Yarmouth. Plagued by financial and other problems, the ECR was forced to abandon its initial aims, and by 29th March, 1843 a much shorter line was in operation from London to Colchester. Meanwhile, the Northern & Eastern had made considerable progress, and a line between London and Bishops Stortford was in operation by 1842. On 1st January, 1844 the Eastern Counties Railway took over the Northern & Eastern on a 999 year lease, and although the original ECR line had still not progressed beyond Colchester, the Northern & Eastern line was extended to Cambridge and Brandon on 29th July, 1845. At Brandon, the ECR line met a line from Norwich, which was opened on the same day by the Norfolk Railway. Itself an amalgam of the Yarmouth & Norwich and Norwich & Brandon, the Norfolk Railway was one of several locally-inspired schemes that had emerged during the 1840s. Such schemes were now coming thick and fast, for the mid-1840s were a time of "Railway Mania" in which companies were floated in a reckless and completely un-coordinated manner.

Other lines promoted at this time included the Lynn & Ely, the Lynn & Dereham, the Lynn & Fakenham, the Eastern Union, the

Newmarket & Chesterford, the Waveney & Gt Yarmouth, and the Wells to Thetford. Of greater significance, as far as Wells was concerned was a proposed extension of the Norfolk Railway from Wymondham to Dereham and thence to Wells and Blakeney; this line, which would meet the Lynn & Dereham at Dereham, was a precursor of the later Wells & Fakenham scheme which eventually succeeded in linking Wells to the Victorian railway system. Unfortunately, the nation was, in 1845, heading towards an economic crisis of unparalleled dimensions, and in the event, many of these projects were doomed to inglorious failure.

By 1847 Britain (not yet a rich country) was investing far more money in railways than it could earn from exports; moreover a series of abysmally wet Summers had led to a partial failure of the corn harvest and a total failure of the potato crop. With so much capital tied-up in railway construction a crisis of some kind was perhaps inevitable, but the collapse, when it came was worse than anyone could have envisaged. Prices spiralled, banks failed, and thousands were thrown out of work; in Ireland and Scotland – even in parts of England – people were starving to death, and against this background of total disaster many wild schemes hatched during the Railway Mania were abandoned.

Developments in the 1840s

Other, more soundly-based projects were hurried to completion, and in these years several important sections of line were opened, including the Eastern Union between Colchester and Ipswich (15th June, 1846), the Ipswich & Bury between Ipswich and Bury St Edmunds (24th December, 1846) and an Eastern Union extension between Haughley and Norwich (12th December, 1849).

In western Norfolk, the Lynn & Ely was opened between Lynn and Downham on 27th October, 1846 and completed throughout to Ely on 25th October, 1847. The Lynn & Dereham reached Narborough on 27th October, 1846 and Sporle (about 2 miles from Swaffham) on 26th October, 1847. In the meantime the Lynn & Ely, Lynn & Dereham and Ely & Huntingdon railways had amalgamated to form the appropriately-named East Anglian Railway. The Norfolk Railway's original Wells scheme had by this time been abandoned, but although the branch was not completed in its entirety, a single track line was opened for goods traffic between Wymondham and Dereham on 7th December, 1846, and for passenger traffic on 15th February, 1847. On 11th September, 1848 the Lynn and Dereham line was opened throughout, placing Dereham in connection with both Norwich and Kings Lynn.

Thus, by 1848, the first section of the Wells branch had been opened as an 11½ mile branch of the Norfolk Railway; the remaining 21½ miles between Dereham and Wells were not yet built, but with work progressing on an extension to Fakenham, there were hopes that the Norfolk Railway would be able to complete its whole scheme at some future date.

Many lines promoted during the heady days of the Railway Mania were so small that they could not remain viable as independent concerns, and for this reason they tended to amalgamate with each other in order to form larger (and hopefully more profitable) organisations. Inevitably, smaller companies such as the Norfolk Railway and the East Anglian Railway gravitated towards larger, more successful concerns – and in this way the Eastern Counties Railway gradually assumed a position of power throughout East Anglia. In 1847 the newly-created East Anglian Railway approached the Eastern Counties Board with a view to amalgamation, but negotiations were unsuccessful on that occasion. An amalgamation with the Norfolk Railway was, on the other hand, immediately attractive to the Eastern Counties directorate, and on 8th May, 1848 they assumed control of the entire Norfolk Railway system (including of course the Wymondham to Dereham line).

Curiously, the Eastern Counties took over its smaller neighbour by mutual arrangement, hoping that Parliament would soon consent to a full amalgamation. Perversely, Parliament refused to sanction this amalgamation, and the ECR Directors were unable to take full possession of the Norfolk Railway – which remained in existence as a separate organisation. However, the Eastern Counties became responsible for all matters relating to operation and day to day running, and by July 1850 all of the Norfolk Railway's locomotives and rolling stock had been purchased by the ECR.

Opening to Fakenham

The Fakenham extension was opened to the public on 20th March, 1849. Heading due north from the existing railhead at Dereham, this 12 mile, single track branch followed the Wensum Valley for much of its length, but civil engineering was nevertheless heavy (at least by East Anglian standards) and there were several deep cuttings. Intermediate stations were provided at Elmham and Ryburgh, and the line was single track throughout. All train services were provided by the Eastern Counties Railway using former Norfolk Railway locomotives and rolling stock.

Unfortunately the Norfolk Railway, having remained in being as an independent company, was soon at odds with the ECR; the 1848 operating agreement was particularly unsuccessful as far as the

WELLS AND FAKENHAM.

A meeting of this company was held on the 15th instant, at the Crown Inn, Wells; the Rev. J. R. HOPPER, in the chair.—The Chairman said the line was completed and the shareholders very naturally wished to see it opened. The town of Wells was not only suffering from the delay which had taken place. but the shareholders were also losing their interest, In passenger traffic alone he believed they were sacrificing 200*l.* per week; and it was quite necessary, therefore, that measures should be taken to expedite the opening of the line.—Mr. Gardner said he felt highly dissatisfied with the course pursued by the directors in not opening the line. About three years and a half had now passed since the first call was paid, and the shareholders had still only got a line to look at for their money. He therefore moved—"That this meeting views with great dissatisfaction the repeated delays in opening this line of railway, and, on behalf of the shareholders generally, at once calls upon the directors to explain the cause of such unnecessary postponement."—Mr. Loynes said he had been unable to procure any satisfactory explanation of the delay which had taken place from the resident director. A promise had been made that the line should be opened as soon as the calls were paid up. The shareholders had performed their part, and had a right to know why the opening was delayed — Mr. Tyrrell said, "hope deferred maketh the heart sick." He believed the hearts of the shareholders had been sick for some time. He begged therefore to move—"That the great delay in not opening this line of railway is highly prejudicial to the interests of this town and district; and that unless steps be immediately taken by the directors to carry out the promise originally made to the shareholders, this meeting will deem it necessary to memorialise the Board of Trade to enforce them to do so."—Mr. Loynes proposed that a letter should be addressed to the directors, calling upon them to state why the line was not opened.—Mr. B J. Everett expressed his opinion that the directors were entitled to credit for the speedy completion of the line, and that there must be some substantial reason for its not having been opened There was a director present, but perhaps his lips were sealed. He thought that, as the Wells people had subscribed manfully for the line, it was very hard that they should not have a prospect of being remunerated as soon as possible.—A letter to the directors stating the grievances of the shareholders, and expressing their determination, in the absence of satisfactory explanations, to seek the interference of the Board of Trade, was then adopted, and an adjournment to 3d August agreed to.—Mr. Southgate, the director present, having been repeatedly requested to afford some *viva voce* explanation, said, as the line was completed, he did not blame the shareholders for demanding the cause of the delay which had taken place. A difficulty had existed between the Eastern Counties directors and the Wells and Fakenham board, but from what he had heard he believed the differences were in a fair way of being settled. Mr. Love, the chairman of the Eastern Counties, with whom he had had an interview, was a thorough man of business; and he felt sure the increase of traffic which the Wells and Fakenham would bring to the Eastern Counties would induce Mr. Love to meet them in an equitable manner.

A press report of the Half year meeting held at Wells on 15th July, 1857.

branch was concerned and the Norfolk Railway Directors complained that local services were "practically useless". It seems that the Eastern Counties timetable was geared towards main line rather than branch operation, and in an attempt to remedy this situation the Norfolk Railway undertook to work some local branch services independently of the ECR. A few of the engines previously sold to the Eastern Counties were therefore transferred back to the Norfolk Railway, the new compromise agreement coming into force in May 1851; within a few months, however, the ECR had once again assumed control of all train services on the Norfolk Railway.

Formation of the Wells & Fakenham

The failure of the original Norfolk Railway scheme had obviously caused great disappointment in Wells-next-the-Sea, but the townsfolk still hoped that with a rail link of their own they would be able to develop as a modern sea port, catering for both commercial vessels and an expanded fishing fleet. A railway would also help the Earl of Leicester and his tenants – enabling locally-grown produce to reach wider markets than had hitherto been possible. There was therefore a unanimity of opinion that Wells needed a railway of its own, and when it became clear that neither the Norfolk Railway nor the Eastern Counties was prepared to extend their existing line any nearer than Fakenham, the people of Wells-next-the-Sea decided to form their own, locally-based company as a means of securing the desired rail link.

The decision to form the "Wells & Fakenham Railway" was probably taken behind the closed doors of Holkham Hall, and it seems clear that Thomas William Coke (1822–1909) was a prime supporter of the scheme. The son of "Coke of Norfolk", T.W. Coke had succeeded to the Holkham estates on the death of his father in 1842. A dedicated "improver", he had already done much to enhance the value of Holkham and the surrounding lands – one of his improvements being the long "sea wall" or embankment running due north from Wells quay and enclosing an area of reclaimed salt marsh; a rail link to the outside world would be a natural corollary of these improvement schemes. Other major landowners interested in the new railway included Sir Willoughby Jones and Lord Hastings. Support from the Norfolk and Eastern Counties railways would be essential, and when in the 1850s the Wells & Fakenham promoters held a series of public meetings in the area, they already had the backing of the Norfolk Railway, and several of its Directors.

It was agreed that the new railway would run southwards from Wells to an end-on junction with the existing railway at Fakenham; the proposed line would be 9½ miles long, and follow the Stiffkey

Valley for much of its length. An Act for the "Wells & Fakenham Railway" was obtained on 24th July, 1854 (17 & 18 Vic. cap. 180), the newly-incorporated company having an authorised capital of £70,000. Unfortunately, Parliament had not allowed the Norfolk Railway to subscribe directly, but in practice this apparent obstacle was overcome when a group of individual Norfolk Railway Directors themselves subscribed £30,000. Local subscribers included the Earl of Leicester, who provided the respectable sum of £10,000, and a group of Wells traders who were able to raise a further £14,000 on behalf of the town itself. Other supporters of the scheme included Sir Willoughby Jones, Joseph Springhill Southgate, Sir Samuel Morton Peto, J.H. Gurney, Hall William Keary, Richard Till, Horatio Bolingbroke and Jacob Watson.

Some of these gentlemen were, like their patron the Earl of Leicester, local landowners or traders who sincerely believed that Wells needed its own rail link; others were representatives of the Norfolk Railway with little obvious interest in the new line, while one or two individuals may have been speculative investors, seeking a return on their initial outlay. There was nevertheless a "hard core" of fully-committed supporters, led by H.W. Keary of Holkham, J.S. Southgate of Wells – and of course the Earl himself.

Horatio Bolingbroke and Richard Till were both representatives of the Norfolk Railway, Mr Till being its Chairman. Of greater significance was the interest initially shown by J.H. Gurney – a member of the famous East Anglian banking family – and Sir Samuel Morton Peto (1809–1889). Peto, in partnership with Edward Ladd Betts, had already constructed much of the East Anglian railway system. As a contractor (rather than a financier or engineer) he had already earned enough money to set himself up as a country gentleman at Somerleyton Hall – just over the county border in Suffolk; both Peto and Gurney were representatives of the Norfolk Railway, and as well as being major subscribers, they were able to act as a useful link between the Norfolk and Wells & Fakenham companies.

Sadly, Peto was a man who liked to play a leading role in as many projects as he could, and in view of his immense wealth he rapidly insinuated himself into a dominant position on the Wells & Fakenham Board, becoming its Chairman and using the little company as a mere pawn in his own private schemes – which in any case centred on Lowestoft rather than Wells-next-the-Sea. In retrospect, Peto's apparent duplicity did nothing but harm to the Wells & Fakenham Railway, and one senses that the most-committed Wells Directors such as Joseph Springhill Southgate, Hall William Keary and Richard Till rued the day that Samuel Morton Peto became involved with their modest, but entirely laudable railway scheme. All of this, however, was in the future, and in the meantime Messrs Peto, Keary and Southgate focused their thoughts on the immediate task of constructing the railway.

With commendable caution the Wells & Fakenham promoters had decided that work would not begin until land had been obtained on reasonable terms, but this was not in the event a major problem and one assumes that Thomas Coke was able to persuade his fellow-landowners that the railway would be a means of improving local agriculture. Happily, the landowners offered "every facility" to the Wells & Fakenham promoters and there was no difficulty in obtaining possession of land for the stations and track bed. Meanwhile, the Norfolk Railway had agreed to work the branch on unusually generous terms, with only 46 per cent of the gross receipts being paid to the operating company. On the other hand the Norfolk Railway had cleverly persuaded the Wells & Fakenham to agree that compensation might be paid if traffic was lost south of Fakenham as a result of the new link to Wells harbour (where a system of quayside lines was already planned).

The rank and file shareholders were told about their new operating agreement at the half-yearly meeting held at Wells on 15th August, 1855. Peto, in the chair, explained that only 46 per cent would be paid to the Norfolk railway, and went on to paint a highly-roseate picture of the future. "The line", he said, "would pass through a rich agricultural district", while the port of Wells, he claimed, "possessed great capabilities". Moving on to the technicalities of construction, the Chairman told his delighted shareholders that of 87 acres needed for the new railway, no less than 58 had been purchased; a line would be fenced-off "as soon as the corn was off the ground", and although the station sites had not been finally settled "there would be one at Walsingham".

Problems and Delays

Having obtained their Act, arranged a favourable operating agreement with the Norfolk Railway, and solved the potentially-thorny problem of land acquisition, the Wells & Fakenham Directors must have assumed that the remainder of their task would be easy, but sadly, this was not to be, and the local company soon found itself at the centre of quarrels that were not of its making. As we have seen, the Eastern Counties Railway had, in the 1840s, emerged as a major force in East Anglian Railway politics. In the longer term, this ambitious company would ultimately be transformed into the Great Eastern Railway, but in the meantime its devious ways and questionable tactics caused much disquiet. One of the Eastern Counties Board's first actions, on taking control of the Norfolk Railway in 1848, had been the dismissal of most former Norfolk Railway staff – and there were, as we have seen, loud complaints about the way in which the ECR ran its trains. Having paid out dividends from much needed capital, the Eastern Counties soon found itself in dire financial straights, and the company's reputation was not helped by two unpleasant Boardroom revolts (one in 1849 and another in 1856).

The Eastern Counties Railway was, by any definition, an exceedingly disreputable organisation – yet this same company was, through its operating agreement with the Norfolk Railway, ultimately responsible for the Wells-next-the-Sea branch! This was clearly a recipe for disaster, and it was perhaps no real surprise that the ECR started to put pressure on the Norfolk Railway over the Wells & Fakenham operating agreement. In 1856 the Eastern Counties declared that the operating agreement could not be considered in any way binding until the Board of Trade had approved.

This rather high-handed action appeared to be blatant obstructionism, and suspicious minds wondered if the Eastern Counties was jealous of its monopoly at Lowestoft – where huge sums had been spent in the hope that a major international trade could be developed; if Wells was allowed to develop as a rival port the Lowestoft investment would be jeopardised. Significantly, Samuel Morton Peto was one of those attempting to promote Lowestoft and the railways leading to it, and none of these factors boded well for the Wells & Fakenham Railway.

Norwich and Brandon Railway.

Length 38 miles. 10 passenger and goods stations. Commences at Norwich, in junction with the Yarmouth and Norwich Railway; and terminates at Brandon, in junction with the extension of the Northern and Eastern Railway, with a branch to Thetford. Passes through the Counties of Norfolk and Suffolk. Gauge of way 4 feet 8½ inches. Royal Assent given to Bill, 16th May, 1844. Half-yearly Meetings, February and August, in London. Opened throughout July, 1845. Fares from London to Norwich, First Class, 22s. 6d. Second Class, 16s. Third Class, 10s. 6d.

Amalgamated with the Yarmouth and Norwich Railway under the title of the Norfolk Railway. Act passed June 30th, 1845, and have also obtained an Act for an extension to Diss and Dereham, 17 miles,

Capital Account.

19,000 Shares, 20*l*. each; 16*l*. Paid. Whole Shares.
19,000 Shares, 10*l*. each; 1*l*. Paid. New Shares.

Total sum authorised to be raised by Shares	380,000*l*.
Ditto ditto by loan or mortgage .	126,000*l*
Total sum expended to June, 1845	314,777*l*.

Railway Shareholder's Manual of 1843 by Henry Tuck.

Chapter Two

Early Years of the Wells & Fakenham Railway (1857–1862)

Undeterred by the problems which now faced them the Wells Directors pressed on with their scheme, and contracts for construction of the line were signed in September 1855; by 1856 the work had begun in earnest under the direction of George Berkeley – an experienced, though perhaps little-known engineer. The physical tasks were relatively easy, though not without problems – one of the most testing being at East Barsham, where the authorised route spanned a deep marshy valley. Berkeley's solution was unusual, though by no means unique – he built an American-style timber trestle viaduct as an alternative to a more expensive embankment; such structures were cheap to build, and could always be replaced at some later date. Apart from its viaduct, the Wells & Fakenham route necessitated considerable earthworks, including a deep cutting at Fakenham and a tunnel at East Barsham (this tunnel was, interestingly enough, one of only two in Norfolk – the other being at Cromer).

The Cost of the Railway

The 9½ mile long, single track railway was completed by June 1857, the entire project having been accomplished in the creditable time of 20 months. Moreover, the Wells & Fakenham was built at an approximate cost of £70,000 – as had been forecast when the company was incorporated. The company's published accounts provide a

Table 1
EXPENDITURE TO 30th JUNE, 1857

	£	s.	d.
Construction of the railway	31,097	0	10
Permanent way materials	18,456	11	8
Purchase of land	8,950	19	0
Act of incorporation	2,597	11	3
Erection of stations	4,531	12	9
Engineering & surveying fees	2,091	0	6
Law charges	1,853	4	2
Directors' fees	750	0	0
Salaries & office charges	466	15	5
Compensation to tenants	394	7	4
Travelling expenses	227	16	2
Advertising, printing & stationery	120	15	8
Rates, taxes & auditors' fees	59	7	7
TOTAL EXPENDITURE	£71,597	2*s*	4*d*

valuable insight into how this sum was spent; it is interesting to note, for example, that the Act alone cost over £2,500 – and one wonders how the Directors spent their £750 "fees" (obviously not on travelling because this item is listed separately!). The relevant section of the Wells & Fakenham accounts is reproduced in **Table 1**:

Although the railway was substantially complete by the Summer of 1857 it could not be opened to traffic until the tedious legal wrangling over operating agreements had been sorted out. Those who had subscribed to the scheme were dismayed to find that trains were not yet able to reach Wells, and the half-yearly meeting held at the Crown Inn, Wells on 15th July, 1857 was a particularly stormy affair. Most Directors failed to appear and in their absence the chair was taken by the Rev. J.R. Hopper.

Continued "Difficulties"

Opening the meeting, the Reverend gentleman sympathised with the shareholders, stating that their line was complete but not in operation, and in the meantime Wells was suffering as a result of the delay while the shareholders were losing interest. In passenger traffic alone, he believed, they were sacrificing £200 per week, and it was necessary therefore that measures should be taken to "expedite the opening of the line". One by one, the angry shareholders voiced their complaints – much of odium falling upon Joseph Southgate, the only Director brave enough to turn up; a Mr Everitt was particularly vociferous, suggesting that there was "some substantial reason" for

157.—GREAT EASTERN.

Incorporated by 25 and 26 Vic., cap. 223 (7th August, 1862), and comprising the EASTERN COUNTIES, NORFOLK, EASTERN UNION, EAST ANGLIAN, EAST SUFFOLK, and other subsidiary undertakings in connection therewith.

I. EASTERN COUNTIES, which is mainly formed of two arteries—the one to Colchester, and the other to Cambridge; the first was incorporated by 6 and 7 Wm. IV., cap. 106 (1836), for a railway from London to Norwich and Yarmouth, by Romford, Chelmsford, Colchester, and Ipswich. Owing, however, to difficulties in raising the requisite funds, the original scheme was not carried beyond Colchester, 51 miles from London.

WELLS AND FAKENHAM.—Incorporated by 17 and 18 Vic., cap. 180 (24th July, 1854). The line (10 miles) was promoted by residents in the districts, who determined to obtain possession of the land at reasonable prices before commencing the works. Capital, 70,000*l*. in 20*l*. shares; power to borrow extends to 23,000*l*. Opened December 1st, 1857. By 22 and 23 Vic., cap. 139 (13th August, 1859), the company was authorised to extend the line along the quay, at Wells, to raise additional capital to the extent of 3,800*l*. at 6 per cent. preference, with loan of 1,200*l*., and to convert the debenture debt into stock. By the same Act the Norfolk may guarantee interest or dividend on the new capital of 3,800*l*., provided the annual net revenue will so permit.

Extract from Bradshaw's Shareholder's Manual.

the continued delay. Eyeing Mr Southgate, he admitted that the Directors deserved credit for the speedy completion of their line, but the people of Wells had "subscribed manfully" to the scheme and it was very hard that they "should not have the prospect of being remunerated as soon as possible".

After repeated questioning Mr Southgate finally spoke to the meeting; he did not, he said, blame them for demanding explanations for the delay that had taken place, but there was a "difficulty" between the Eastern Counties Directors and the Wells & Fakenham Board. However "from what he had heard" he believed that these differences would soon be settled; Mr Love, the Eastern Counties Chairman was, he suggested, "a thorough man of business" who would meet them in "an equitable manner" when he realised that extra traffic would be brought to the Eastern Counties system once the Wells & Fakenham was open.

At the root of these "difficulties" was the 46 per cent operating agreement between the Wells & Fakenham and Norfolk companies which the Eastern Counties (as operating company) had no intention of honouring; it was in effect a three cornered battle between the Wells & Fakenham, Norfolk and Eastern Counties – though much speculation centred around the precise role of Sir Samuel Morton Peto. The Editor of *The Railway Times* was not afraid to publicly accuse Peto of duplicity, and on 29th August, 1857 this influential investors' journal considered the Wells & Fakenham's problems in a leading article. The paper noted that Peto had undertaken "to secure the working of the line at 46 per cent, the Norfolk being the instrument by which that engagement was intended to be fulfilled". However, the Norfolk Railway "by the *instrumentality of Sir Morton Peto*", was then handed over to the Eastern Counties, and as matters stood, the Eastern Counties Board were under no obligation to work the Wells & Fakenham. Having in effect accused Peto of double dealing, *The Railway Times* suggested a possible solution to the Wells & Fakenham problem:

> If Sir Morton were called to account by the Wells & Fakenham, the worthy baronet could call the Norfolk to account for breach of the agreement he made in its name and on its behalf . . . It is admitted on all hands that the traffic on the Wells & Fakenham cannot be worked at 46 per cent, yet it was on the faith of that representation being carried through that the line was made. It is obvious therefore that there are other partners to be dealt with than the Eastern Counties, and that it is in no degree surprising that Mr Till of the Norfolk should advise patience in the first instance, and a short agreement with the Eastern Counties in the second, so that the chapter of accidents may be taken advantage of rather than the original prospectus should be brought under review.

In the end, the Wells & Fakenham Directors (or rather those who wanted to see the railway in operation) were forced to go cap in hand to the Eastern Counties and accept whatever terms the larger company might offer. There were still three or four loyal Directors willing to stand up for the unfortunate Wells & Fakenham – including Joseph Southgate, Hall William Keary and (perhaps surprisingly) Richard Till of the Norfolk Railway. Southgate and Keary, being local men, were understandably keen to see the railway in operation, but it is harder to see why Mr Till should have fought so hard on behalf of the Wells company – other than perhaps his own sense of honour; a wrong had been done and it was therefore a matter of duty that things should be put right.

Whatever behind-the-scenes "rescue package" was concocted, the loyal Directors still had to convince their shareholders, and under these circumstances the half-yearly meeting held in August 1857 was expected to be another lively affair. In an attempt to defuse the situation the Directors held this crucial meeting not in Wells but at Fakenham – hoping perhaps that, with the railway not yet in operation, a smaller number of shareholders would attend! (If indeed this was the case, their ploy was highly successful, and the meeting was poorly-attended and relatively placid.)

The meeting was chaired by Hall Keary, and the first report was read by Mr Hutt the company Secretary. Although there was no immediate prospect of opening, the Secretary was able to report at least some progress:

> The Directors have the satisfaction to announce that your line of railway between Wells and Fakenham, with the stations and works, has been completed with the exception of the harbour branch now in progress and a tramway which your Directors, at the earnest solicitation of some of the principal shareholders and merchants of the town of Wells, had undertaken to construct along the quay, but which has not been commenced in consequence of objections raised by one of the owners of property past which it was proposed the intended tram should be carried. The opening of the main line is now only delayed for the completion of a junction with the lines of the Eastern Counties and Norfolk at Fakenham and the necessary arrangements for station accommodation there, and for working the line; but your Directors are actively negotiating with the other companies and trust in a short time satisfactorily to effect those objects. Should they be disappointed in this anticipation, your Directors will immediately call a special meeting of the shareholders to consider and determine the course to be pursued. The account of capital received and expended to the 30th June last has already been printed and sent to every shareholder in the usual way.

The Secretary then read a report submitted by George Berkeley, the company Engineer:

> I beg to report that the works on the main line between Fakenham and the passenger station at Wells are complete, with the exception of a short length of about one hundred yards, near the Fakenham station, where possession of the land which is now occupied by the Eastern Counties and used in working their traffic has not yet been obtained. The execution of the works on this land, where possession is obtained, will not occupy more than ten days or a fortnight. The earthworks, etc., on the goods branch to the water-side at Wells are rapidly progressing and this branch may be completed as soon as the main line can be opened for public traffic.

Hall William Keary apologised for the continued delay in opening the railway, pointing out that the line had been built within its time limit, and would have been in operation had not other matters interfered. Trying to sound optimistic he emphasised that "a very excellent line of railway" had been made to "the seaport town of Wells", and added that negotiations which had been "long pending" between the Wells & Fakenham and Eastern Counties were at last "drawing to a favourable conclusion". He then said a few words on behalf of Richard Till, who had clearly done his utmost to get the railway opened:

> I am glad to see on my right hand Mr Till, the Chairman of the Norfolk, who has throughout conducted the negotiations in a most able manner, and to whom we are much indebted for the position at which we are now arrived. I believe he will be able to explain to you most satisfactorily that nothing has been wanting on our part to fulfil our duties towards you, and that we have taken every step that we could to bring difficult negotiations to a favourable conclusion. I beg to say, as I said before, that if you require any further explanation I am quite sure our friend Mr Till will be most happy to give it.

There were, needless to say, one or two questions – notably from the vociferous Mr Everitt who challenged the accounts. Why, he asked "was something like £3,000 still unpaid on the tenth call?" The Directors replied that this was in fact owed by the Norfolk Railway, but as the Wells & Fakenham was itself in debt to the Norfolk "it would have been a useless proceeding to have paid the money over under such circumstances". Finally, Richard Till rose to speak, and the assembled shareholders listened attentively as the Norfolk Railway Chairman delivered a mixture of good and bad news:

> The Chairman has referred to me, in consequence of the disappointment which the proprietors naturally feel when, after having laid out their money in the formation of their railway it is not immediately opened and turned to good account. It is one of those difficulties which frequently present themselves when a small independent company have created a branch and have to deal with an old constituted company who have pretty

well the power in their hands. We are certainly more than unfortunate with respect to the company with which we have had to negotiate, because that company, prior to the last half year, have been in a state of change and transition, one body of Directors going out and another body of Directors going in.

Mr Till was here referring to the forced resignation of David Waddington (1810–1863), the ECR Chairman; an associate of George Hudson, he had been more interested in railway politics than in running trains, and under his Chairmanship the Wells & Fakenham stood little chance of getting a fair deal. The Wells Directors clearly hoped that Horatio Love, the new ECR Chairman, would come "to reasonable and fair terms" *vis-à-vis* the Wells & Fakenham, and Mr Till seemed relatively optimistic as he continued his speech:

Of late a better feeling has come over the negotiations . . . and . . . I see no difficulty now in coming to a final arrangement with the Eastern Counties. Unfortunately, we first made an arrangement with the Norfolk, who were desirous to receive the traffic and make arrangements which would give us a fair proportion of the advantages which would accrue from the line to both parties. Before, however, the line was finished, and before it was ripe for a final settlement of the negotiations, the Norfolk, under a special agreement, made over the whole of their property to the management of the Eastern Counties, for the benefit of the three allied companies. This, as you may easily suppose, has presented a certain amount of difficulty, which would not have occurred if this company had treated only with the Norfolk. But we must take things as they are, and as we find them, and do the best we can. Things have now come to this – the Chairman of the Eastern Counties has intimated to me that he is authorised to bring the matter to a final close, and this company has done me the honour to authorise me on their part to settle it. The Eastern Counties have appointed their Engineer to settle and arrange with the gentleman appointed by us – that is *our* Engineer – the terms upon which the junction shall take place, and as far as I am able to understand from our Engineer the matter is approaching very closely to a conclusion. I should hope within a week there will be an announcement of the terms these two gentlemen recommend; and if they differ, that they will get some third party to decide between them. A matter affecting the Norfolk, over which the Eastern Counties have no control, has been adjusted in the most friendly way, a proper and efficient person having been appointed as valuer, to settle the sum this company should pay to the Norfolk for possession of their property from the first bridge up to the junction with the Wells & Fakenham line proper. The only difficulty to be arranged was, that so much of the land as in the occupation and use of the allied companies from the bridge up to the Fakenham station should become the property of this company, that we might have under any circumstances a positive approach which should not be interfered with to the Fakenham station. Then, instead of spending our money uselessly in building a fresh

> station, we have to settle the annual amount to be paid for the use of the Fakenham station with respect to our traffic. There is a third point of more difficulty, namely, the terms upon which the Eastern Counties will work our traffic; but if any confidence is to be placed in the assertions of the Chairman of that company, he is willing to settle the matter upon fair and reasonable terms . . . if there is any other explanation which I am capable of affording I am quite at your service.

The meeting ended with a question-and-answer session – the main questioner being the irrepressible Mr Everitt who seemed particularly concerned with the 46 per cent operating agreement; he was obviously quite right to persist for Mr Till had been unable or unwilling to go into this matter in detail. In fact, there was no hope of the Eastern Counties working the line on anything like favourable terms, and when the matter was finally sorted out the terms were hardly congenial. The Directors must by this time have known that they would have to give way to the ECR – though one feels that they were reluctant to reveal all to their unfortunate shareholders.

Opening of the Wells & Fakenham

As the Summer of 1857 turned to Autumn, the Wells & Fakenham Directors at last turned their thoughts towards public opening – which was initially planned for 1st October, 1857 but finally took place on 1st December exactly six months after the works had been completed.

The Great Day was celebrated in style, and having dipped into their own pockets to provide appropriate festivities, the townsfolk of Wells-next-the-Sea were determined that a good time would be had by all. Opening Day was declared a public holiday, and many hundreds gathered at Wells and along the lineside to witness the first official trains. The streets of the little town were elaborately decorated with flags, bunting and triumphal arches of evergreens, and – on an odd note – a band of "Norwich widows" was hired to provide musical accompaniment. The first train was greeted by tumultuous cheering and a fusillade from the muskets of local Coast Guards. Later, the customary speeches of congratulation were made after a banquet held in the Crown Inn, while the commonalty celebrated outside by the light of bonfires and flaring tar barrels!

Early Years

The new railway was worked by the Eastern Counties as a nine and a half mile extension of the Norfolk Railway branch from Fakenham. There was an intermediate station at Walsingham, and the original train service provided just four trains each way; one of these was a "mixed" working conveying both passenger and freight vehicles. At Wells the line terminated away from the quays in the older part of the town, but in 1859 the Wells & Fakenham Directors belatedly completed their short goods branch to Wells quay and, when opened, this useful facility enabled ships to discharge their cargoes directly into waiting railway wagons.

In practice, the ketches, barges and schooners which tied-up at Wells quay tended to *compete* with the railway – though it was not unknown when vessels were stormbound (or held-up by adverse winds) for shipowners to transfer cargoes onto the railway as a means of ensuring prompt delivery. Corn, destined for export via Wells harbour, may have been sent down to the quays by train – but local farmers would have used their cream or blue-coloured "Norfolk" wagons for shorter distance journeys. The quayside branch was nevertheless a useful addition to the system, and it obviously attracted at least some extra freight traffic to the Wells & Fakenham Railway.

Sadly, the new railway did not prosper, and although its initial receipts had equalled the "most sanguine expectations" of the Directors, receipts for the first six months equalled only £1,656 – whereas expenditure totalled £1,774. Moreover, the Eastern Counties did nothing to ease the lot of the local company, and the Wells & Fakenham Directors suspected that they were being swindled. At the half-year meeting held at Wells in September 1859, for example, Hall Keary complained that the ECR was working the line at 55 per cent and "would not co-operate on *fair* terms". A revenue account had been rendered by the Eastern Counties, but (he added darkly) it "*had not yet been investigated*".

Six months later the company had still been "unable to effect any satisfactory arrangement with the Eastern Counties for working the line" and receipts for the half year ending 31st December, 1859 had amounted to just £1,846; expenses, including interest, had been £1,749 over the same period. Under these unhappy circumstances, the owners of the little railway seem to have lost heart, and when the time finally came to sell-up, Messrs Keary and Southgate probably felt that a heavy load was soon to be lifted from their shoulders. It would at this point be useful to turn once again to the Eastern Counties in order to understand the events leading up to the Great Eastern takeover.

The End of Local Control

In 1862, the process by which the Eastern Counties Railway acquired control of its smaller neighbours culminated in what was perhaps a long-overdue amalgamation, and on 7th August an Act to "amalgamate the Eastern Counties, the East Anglian, the Newmarket, the Eastern Union and the Norfolk Railway companies" received the Royal Assent. Although in effect the ECR had simply absorbed lines which it already worked, the company wisely decided to rename itself "The Great Eastern Railway" – thereby establishing in the public eye a new organisation which (hopefully) would not be tainted by the abysmal reputation of its immediate predecessor.

These momentous events suggested a solution to the Wells & Fakenham's problems, and the local Directors were only too glad to see their undertaking merged with the Norfolk, the Eastern Counties and other neighbouring companies; in June 1862 Hall Keary and Joseph Southgate announced that the Wells & Fakenham would be "transferred to and vested by amalgamation in the Great Eastern Railway". The last meeting of the company was held at Wells in the following September, and in a conscious attempt to underline the historic nature of the occasion, the chair was taken by Thomas Coke, Earl of Leicester.

It was sad but appropriate that the man who had done so much for the railway in its early years should have had the last word just eight years later; the Earl stated simply that "the property would be vested in the Great Eastern, and the proprietors would receive the amount to be allowed for the property in Great Eastern 4½ per cent Preference Stock in accordance with terms agreed to in the Spring". A general discussion followed, but it was generally agreed that the long-suffering Directors had secured the best possible terms; the debentures would "stand in their integrity" although it was noted that 55 per cent was to be written off ordinary stocks. So ended the short, troubled career of the Wells & Fakenham Railway – an innocent victim of a vicious power struggle waged by the likes of Samuel Morton Peto, David Waddington, and other Victorian capitalists whose primary aim was the acquisition of wealth and power at the expense of any who stood in their way.

The newly-created Great Eastern Railway soon earned an improved reputation, and although the stigma of its Eastern Counties origins remained for many years the reconstituted company eventually became something of an institution throughout East Anglia – an object of pride rather than derision! This change of ownership is unlikely to have bothered the people of Wells, and their branch functioned successfully as part of a 43¼ mile route from Norwich. The completed railway was of considerable benefit to East Dereham – which developed as a rural manufacturing centre after the opening of its rail links.

Wells itself, however,failed to develop in any material way; as we shall see, the town never became a holiday resort, but more surpri-

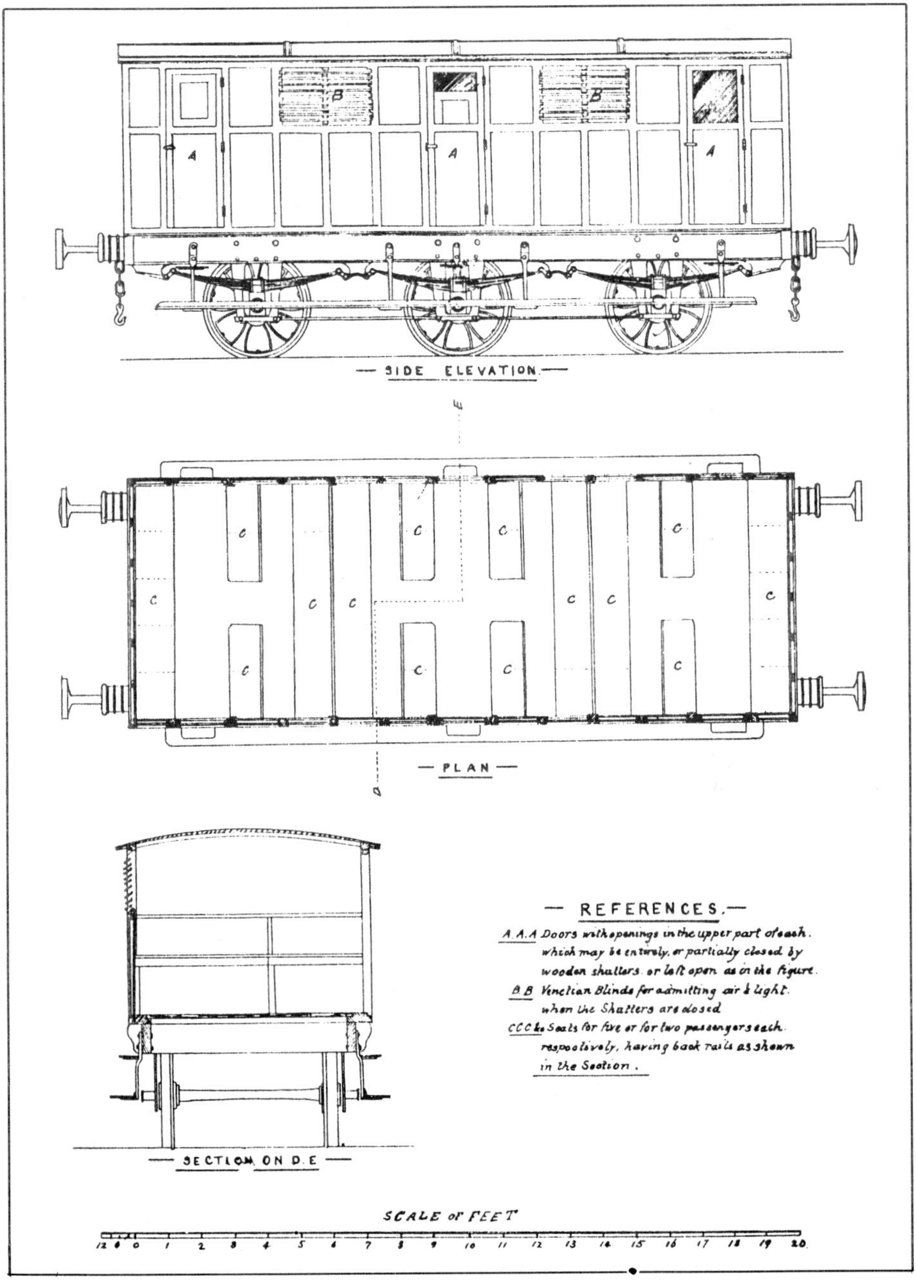

Early Eastern Counties coach similar to those in use on the Norfolk Railway c.1840.

singly, it also failed to prosper as a port. The Great Eastern was not inclined to promote Wells at the expense of its other ports at Kings Lynn, Lowestoft and Harwich, but worse than this, environmental changes along the north Norfolk coast precluded the development of any *large scale* fishing industry. (It had seemed at one time that mussel or oyster fishing might be cultivated off the north Norfolk coast, but storms, and the scouring action of east-west currents seem to have been a major problem.) Moreover, Wells had only 9 ft of water at high tide, and its harbour channel was continually shifting – such a port was far from ideal in the age of sail when vessels had no engines to facilitate manoeuvring in an intricate channel.

The West Norfolk Branch

In spite of these problems local squires and landowners still hoped that Wells and the surrounding coastal area could be developed, and to this end the grandly-named West Norfolk Junction Railway was floated in the 1860s. The new line was to run due west from Wells and, if successful, would encourage fishing and tourism in hitherto remote settlements such as Brancaster, Burnham Market and Docking. At Heacham, the suggested route would join the Lynn & Hunstanton branch – thereby opening up a new route from Wells to Kings Lynn. Supporters of the West Norfolk scheme included Major Humphrey John Hare of Docking, Edward Durrant of Kings Lynn, Edward Self of Kings Lynn, and Lightly Simpson of London; all of these gentlemen were intimately connected with the Lynn & Hunstanton Railway, and as far as can be ascertained none had any obvious link with the Wells & Fakenham.

The West Norfolk Junction obtained its Act on 23rd June, 1864 and the scheme's promoters lost little time in putting their plans into effect. From Wells (where trains would utilise the Wells & Fakenham station) the authorised route ran due west via Holkham, Burnham Market, Stanhoe, Docking and Sedgeford, following the coast as far as Burnham and then bearing inland for the remaining 11 miles. It was initially proposed that triangular junctions would be provided at both Wells and Heacham, but in the event this part of the plan was not completed. Capital of £75,000 was authorised, together with loans of £25,000; a proportion of the capital was subscribed by the GER which undertook to work the train service between Wells and Heacham in return for 50 per cent of the gross receipts.

It was reported, at the half-yearly WNJn meeting held at Kings Lynn in February 1865, that "the works had been carried on with great expedition"; indeed, progress had been so rapid that the Directors hoped to open their line as far as Holkham before the end of the year. This forecast was somewhat optimistic, but it is interesting to note that a Royal Special worked over the uncompleted branch in the early days of 1866; the Royal Train was halted at Burnham Market, at which point the Prince and Princess of Wales alighted for the remainder of their journey to Holkham Hall (where they were spending the New Year while their own house at Sandringham was being rebuilt). The West Norfolk branch was opened for public traffic on 17th August, 1866, thereby opening-up a second route to Wells-next-the-Sea and effectively doubling the amount of traffic handled at Wells.

There were, in general, four trains each way between Wells and Heacham, rising to five on Saturdays and market days; most services terminated at Heacham, but there was usually one through working to Hunstanton which continued northwards after reversal at the junction. Freight services consisted of one return working between Kings Lynn and Wells. These modest services remained unchanged for many years, the amount of traffic offering itself being so small that additional trains would have been superfluous. Receipts were correspondingly low, but unlike the Wells & Fakenham the West Norfolk company struggled on as an independent company until 1874 – when it was merged with the Lynn & Hunstanton Railway to form the "Hunstanton & West Norfolk Railway". (The Hunstanton & West Norfolk was itself sold to the GER in 1890.)

Motive Power in the Early Days

It is impossible to say, with any degree of accuracy, which classes of locomotive were used on the Wells branch during its very early years, but it is nevertheless possible, by a process of elimination to suggest the kind of engines which *might* have appeared. When in 1848 the Norfolk Railway first placed itself under Eastern Counties control, the company possessed just thirty-seven locomotives – most of which were of the ungainly "long boiler" type. Built by Stephensons, Jones & Potts and other specialist manufacturers, they included several 0–6–0 goods engines, some 2–2–2s, and ten 2–4–0s. It is reasonable to assume that most of these engines remained on their own section long after the ECR takeover – the usual practice being for elderly main line locomotives to be demoted to secondary duties when more modern motive power became available on "top link" services.

It is tempting to conclude that former Norfolk Railway 2–4–0s worked on the Wells branch around the time of its opening; as tender engines, they would have the necessary fuel capacity for the 87 mile round journey between Wells and Norwich, while their 5 ft 7 in. wheels would have been ideal for passenger duties. Numbered from 130 to 139 in the ECR locomotive list, they had 15 in. x 22 in. outside cylinders and weighed 23 tons 12 cwt. Some of the class were later

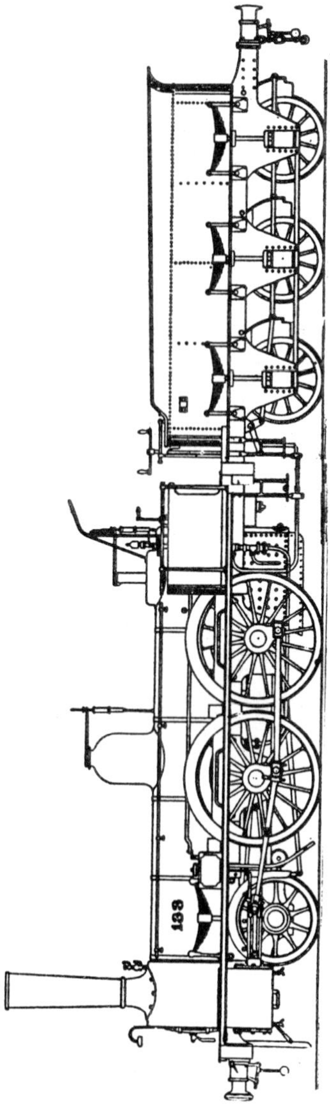

A long boiler 2–4–0 of the Sinclair era; this locomotive was built for the Norfolk Railway in 1847 and scrapped by the GER in 1877.

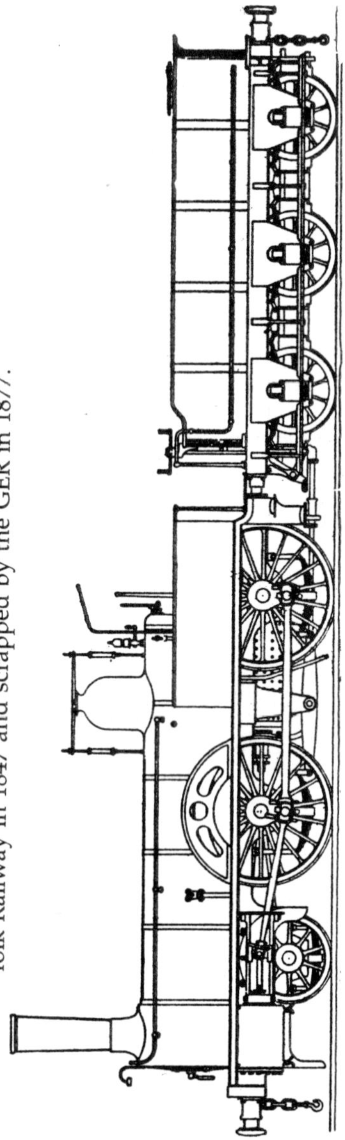

A class 'Y' 2–4–0 locomotive as introduced in the 1860s. Some of this class possessed cabs and had domes placed further forward on the boiler.

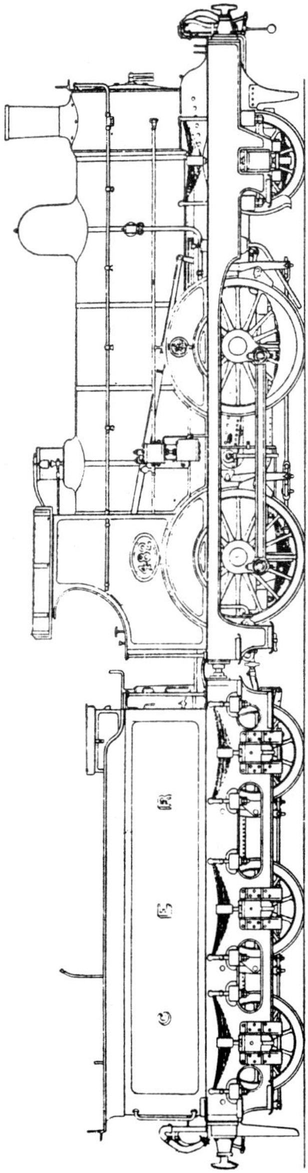

GER 'T26' 2–4–0 No. 482 (later class 'E4')

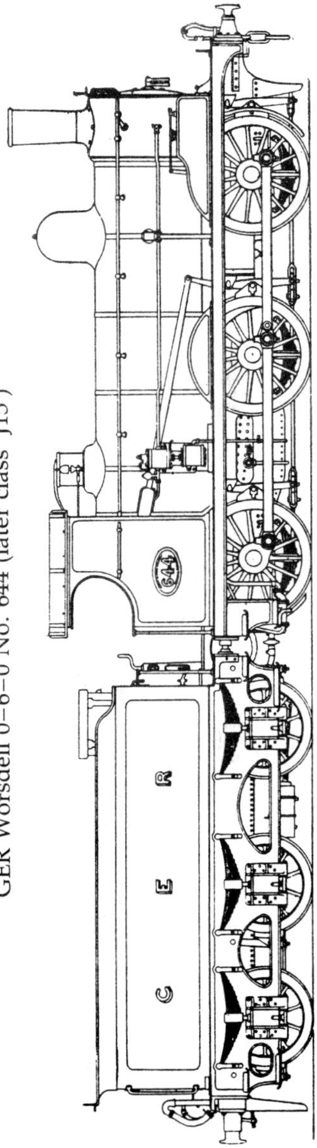

GER Worsdell 0–6–0 No. 644 (later class 'J15')

rebuilt by the ECR, receiving new boilers, stove pipe chimneys and simple weather-boards in place of their earlier open cabs.

The Norfolk Railway also owned three small 2–2–2Ts which had been built specifically for branch line duties, and may therefore have been used on some shorter distance services. Built by E.B. Wilson at the Railway Foundry, Leeds, they had 10 in. x 17 in. inside cylinders, fluted safety valve covers and unusually slender chimneys; probably too small and under-powered for everyday use, they were scrapped at an early date.

Although these suppositions are entirely plausible, recorded locomotive history really begins with the advent of Robert Sinclair's 'Y' class 2–4–0s. Built in batches between 1859 and 1866 there were eventually 110 of these versatile machines at work on the GER, and although originally designed for freight duties they were also used as passenger engines. The 'Y' class had 17 in. x 24 in. cylinders and 6 ft 1 in. coupled wheels; weight, in full working order was approximately 54 tons, and the locomotives were numbered in sequence from 307 to 416.

The relatively long journey between Wells and Norwich dictated the use of tender locomotives rather than tank engines, and for most of its life the branch was worked by various types of 2–4–0 locomotive. These engines were turned at the end of each journey, using a 41 ft 11 in. diameter turntable outside Wells engine shed (this was later replaced by a 45 ft diameter table so that 4–4–0s could be used). There were usually at least two engines shedded at Wells to work the morning up services to Norwich and Heacham respectively; on occasions however there could be three or even four locomotives in the cramped sub-shed at the end of each day's operation.

A Note on Early Liveries and Early Signals

The range of paints available in mid-Victorian years was severely limited in comparison with later periods, and for this reason the predominant colours used on external structures were buff and either brown or green. By analogy with other Victorian lines the Wells & Fakenham would probably have painted its structures in a two tone livery incorporating buff (sometimes described as "stone") and brown; if green was used it would have been a drab mixture known usually as "Holly Green". The constraints governing station colours applied also to locomotives, and it comes as no surprise to find that Eastern Counties/Great Eastern locomotives were adorned – if that is the right word – in a sombre green colour, relieved only by black and red (later white) lining.

In common with other ECR lines the Wells–Wymondham branch would have been signalled with simple, slotted-post semaphores,

GER class T26 2–4–0 No. 492 at Wells-next-the-Sea. (The headcode is for Norwich to Dereham.) *Canon Charles Bayes*

Great Eastern No. 1 class 2–4–0 No. 30 stands beside the tiny water tower at Wells-next-the-Sea; the headcode suggests that the locomotive is about to work through to Norwich. *Canon Charles Bayes*

Great Eastern class T26 2–4–0 No. 420. These engines worked on the Wells branch for many years. *Real Photographs*

Class T26 2–4–0 No. 488. *Real Photographs*

Class E4 No. 7415 leaving Wells-next-the-Sea for Heacham on the 29th June 1936. (The first carriage is a 34 ft 6 in. x 8 ft lavatory third, GER diagram No. 407.) 180 of these were built in 1898/9 of which 171 were still in traffic in August 1936. The last was withdrawn in August 1946. *H.C. Casserley*

An ex-Great Eastern 2–4–2T stands outside the later, brick-built shed at Dereham in 1935. *I. Kite*

Former NER 0–6–0 No. 300 pauses at Dereham station with the 7.16 pm to Norwich (via Wroxham) train on 29th June 1936. *H.C. Casserley*

An ex-Great Eastern class E4 2–4–0 No. 62797 stands outside the goods shed at Wells on 17th June 1951. *L.R. Peters*

Class D13 4–4–0 No. 7707, photographed at Norwich in 1933. These locomotives were, at that time, the largest engines to be seen at Wells-next-the-Sea. *Real Photographs*

Class F3 2–4–2T No. 8088 at Norwich Shed in 1933. *Real Photograph*

Rebuilt class T26 2–4–0 (as class D13 4–4–0 No. 8030) seen here taking water at Wells-next-the-Sea on the 29th June, 1936. *H.C. Casserley*

Class D16/3 "Claud Hamilton" 4–4–0 No. 62577 stands beside the turntable at Wells-next-the-Sea on 15th June 1952. *L.R. Peters*

Class E4 2–4–0 No. 7492 at Dereham on 29th June 1936. (Note the central signal box in background.) *H.C. Casserley*

Class E4 2–4–0 No. 62782 pauses at Dereham station with a local train from Wroxham (via County School); the date is 13th September 1952. *H.B. Priestley*

Fakenham station, looking north, as Claud Hamilton 4–4–0 No. 62577 arrives with a train for Norwich on 1st September 1955. *H.C. Casserley*

Class 31 No. 5633 with the 13.00 service to Norwich, seen here departing from Fakenham station on 6th September 1971. *G.R. Mortimer*

Class 31 No. 5633 arrives at Dereham with a Fakenham to Norwich freight on 6th September 1971. *G.R. Mortimer*

[IMPROVED SAFETY RAILWAY SIGNAL.]

Our illustration shows a signal which can be worked by one man, and with great rapidity. This is effected by turning a handle; and by the same movement of the hand directing either the semaphores by day, or the slides in the lamp by night. This is considered a wonderful improvement over the old system, and we do not doubt, if it came into general use, that it would not only afford some extra protection to the public, but greatly facilitate railway travelling.

An early signal, typical of the type used in the area.

probably supplied by Messrs Stevens & Co. of Darlington Works, Southwark Bridge Road, London. These were worked independently by railwaymen turning a handle near the base of the post, and signal boxes as such did not appear until the later Victorian period. There were, in many cases, two semaphore arms on each post – one for up and the other for down trains, and the operating handle also turned a rotating spindle which, in turn, rotated an oil lamp showing either red or blue-green. The example shown on the previous page is similar to an ECR signal (albeit without the prominently-chamfered post which characterised that company's signals). On closer examination it appears that the vertical spindle changed the lamp from red to green by means of coloured slides; *Measom's Guide to the GER,* showed a similar signal on the Wells branch, with its lamp mounted on an unusually tall spindle-shaft.

WELLS AND FAKENHAM.—The half-yearly meeting was held on 30th ult., at Wells; the Earl of Leicester in the chair, who stated that in the course of the month the property would be vested in the Great Eastern, and the proprietors would receive. the amount to be allowed for the property in Great Eastern 4½ preference stock, in accordance with terms agreed to in the spring. It was expected that the Great Eastern would be enabled to largely develop the traffic, and that the amalgamation would be attended with benefit to the district. Some discussion followed, and the shareholders present appeared to consider that the directors had secured the best terms they could, under which the debentures of the company would stand in their integrity, although 55 per cent. was to be written off the ordinary stock

Contemporary Newspaper cutting of last Wells and Fakenham meeting.

Chapter Three

A Norfolk Branch Line (1862–1923)

Much of the East Anglian railway system had been built piecemeal by a bewildering variety of independent companies, but after the formation of the Great Eastern Railway in 1862 the network developed in a more rational way. The emphasis shifted from the internecine and unregulated competition of the 1840s towards a more rational approach, and in the next few years several more towns and villages were connected to the main system by small (often locally-promoted) branch lines. These lines were usually worked by the Great Eastern – an arrangement which was of benefit to all in so far as the small towns and villages concerned obtained their vital rail links while the GER gained several useful additions to its system. The Norwich–Cromer branch was a typical, locally-based branch line; promoted by the East Norfolk Railway, it was opened from Whitlingham Junction, through Wroxham to North Walsham on 20th October, 1874 and extended northwards to Gunton on 29th July, 1876. Completion to Cromer was accomplished on 26th March, 1877, on which date GER trains began running to yet another Norfolk seaside town.

Victorian Developments

The appearance of the Eastern & Midlands Railway (later the Midland & Great Northern Joint) prompted a further bout of intercompany rivalry at the end of the 1870s, resulting in further additions to the local railway system. The history of the Eastern & Midlands is complex, but briefly, this competitive cross country route originated in the 1860s when three local companies had amalgamated to form the "Midlands & Eastern Railway" – thereby bringing a 36½ mile branch from the Great Northern at Bourne under unified management; in this way the GNR was able to reach Kings Lynn in opposition to the GER. Meanwhile, the opening of a Midland-backed line from Peterborough to Sutton Bridge had brought a third company into the arena, while further east the Lynn & Fakenham and other non-GER interests were actively promoting a tenuous chain of local railways which, when opened at various times between 1877 and 1883, effectively carried the Midlands & Eastern route from Kings Lynn to Great Yarmouth. On 1st August, 1882 the lines east of Kings Lynn were amalgamated as the Eastern & Midlands Railway, and a year later the Eastern & Midlands absorbed the earlier Midlands & Eastern and Peterborough & Sutton Bridge lines. The end result of these complicated amalgamations was a lengthy "main line" from the GNR at Bourne, extending eastwards across GER territory to Great Yarmouth, with branches from Sutton Bridge to Peterborough and from Melton Constable to Norwich; a third branch was later opened from Melton Constable to Cromer.

Understandably alarmed at this blatant threat to its East Anglian heartlands, the Great Eastern promoted new lines of its own – one of which was the Wroxham to County School branch, which joined the Wells route at Broom Green. A classic "political" line, this new section of railway served no obvious economic need. Running for 23 miles 51 chains through sparsely-populated countryside that yielded little or no originating traffic, it was opened in stages, reaching Buxton Lamas on 8th July, 1879 and Aylsham on 1st January, 1880. Although part of the nominally-independent East Norfolk Railway the new line was clearly the Great Eastern's response to the Lynn & Fakenham – which was itself being built in stages just a few miles to the north. The GER route was pushed westwards to reach Cawston on 1st September, 1880, and Reepham by 2nd May, 1881. Finally, on 1st May, 1882 the line was completed throughout to its junction with the Wells branch; there was no station at the actual point of convergence, the "junction" being at County School – a new station which had recently been opened between Elmham and Ryburgh to serve the "Norfolk County School". Meanwhile, the rival Lynn & Fakenham had itself been opened to traffic, though there was no connection whatsoever between the GER and L&F routes at Fakenham – the two stations being on opposite sides of the town.

In 1880 the Lynn & Fakenham obtained Parliamentary consent for a branch from the L&F line at Melton Constable to the coast at Blakeney, and in answer to this further attack on its monopoly in north Norfolk the Great Eastern put forward its own scheme for an extension from Wells to Blakeney. Neither of these lines were ever built – though the Lynn & Fakenham project eventually materialised in a slightly different form as the Eastern & Midlands Railway Cromer branch. (Later, around the turn of the century there was talk of a new GER line from Wells to Holt, but again this interesting scheme was abandoned and Wells-next-the-Sea was destined to remain the terminus of the line until its closure in 1964.)

The growth of East Dereham brought much extra traffic to the southern half of the Wells branch, resulting in the installation of double track between Wymondham and Dereham in the late Victorian period; beyond Dereham however the line remained single, the main crossing loops being at County School and Fakenham. Two freight trains, or one freight and one passenger train, could cross at North Elmham, but the loop at Ryburgh was not used for passing purposes (except possibly in emergencies). Similarly at Walsingham, the sidings could have been used for passing in emergencies, but the

NORWICH, DEREHAM, FAKENHAM, AND WELLS.

UP TRAINS. — WEEK DAYS / SUNDAYS.

Mls. from Wells.	FROM		morn		Mrkt. morn	morn	morn	morn	V even.	even.	W even.	Mkt. Mxd even.	even.	even.	even.			Sun. even.		
	Wells	dep.	6 30	—	—	—	9 8	10 10	12 50	1 50	3 15	even.		6 0		..	—	1 5	—	—
4¾	Walsingham		6 41	—	—	—	9 19	10 21	1 1	●	3 26	—	From Peterboro' and Lynn.	6 11	Tuesdays only.	...	—	1 16	—	—
9¾	**Fakenham**		6 55	—	9 10	9 10	9 23	10 33	1 15	2 11	3 40	4 50		6 24		...	...	1 31	—	—
12¾	Ryburgh		7 1	—	9 16	9 16	9 38	10 39	1 20	●	3 46	4 58		6 30		...	...	1 37	—	—
17¼	North Elmham		7 10	—	9 25	9 25	9 49	10 48	1 31	●	3 57	5 20		6 41		—	—	1 48	—	—
21¼	**Dereham**	arr.	7 19	...	9 34	9 34	9 58	10 57	1 41	2 34	4 8	5 12	5 31	6 50	9 23	...	—	2 0	—	—
		dep.	7 22	Tues. & Sats. only	9 36	9 40	10 2	10 59	1 48	2 36	4 20	Thursdays only.	5 40	6 56	9 35	...	...	2 5	—	—
23¾	Yaxham		7 27		9 41	To Lynn.	—	11 4	1 53	—	4 26			7 1	—	—	—	2 11	—	—
26¼	Thuxton		7 33		9 47		—	11 10	1 59	...	4 31			7 7	...	...	—	2 17	—	—
27¾	Hardingham		7 39		9 52		10 13	11 14	2 4	—	4 36		—	7 12	9 43	...	...	2 22	—	—
29¾	Kimberley		●		9 57		U	11 19	2 9	...	4 41		...	7 17	—	—	...	2 27	—	—
33	**Wymondham**	arr.	7 50	Sats. only.	10 5		10 28	11 27	2 17	2 18	4 50		5 59	7 26	9 59	...	...	2 35	—	—
		dep.	7 51		10 7		10 34	11 30	2 20	2 56	5 5 / 4 52		6 0 / 6 47	7 27	10 0	...	—	2 37	—	—
37	Hethersett		●		10 17		...	11 39	2 29	...	(23) / 5 2		... / ...	7 37	—	...	...	2 47	—	—
42½	Trowse		8 9		10 30		10 41	11 52	2 42	—	/ 5 13		6 16 / —	7 50	10 19	...	—	2 58	—	—
43¼	**Norwich**	arr.	8 14		10 35	—	10 46	11 57	2 47	...	... / 5 20		6 20 /	7 55	10 25	—	...	3 5	—	—
67¼	Cromer	arr.	9 53	...	Via Forncett.	—	12 15	2 32	3 17	Via Forncett.	Via Forncett. / 7 45	—	7 45 / Via Forncett.	9 57	—	—	—	—	—	—
66¾	Lowestoft	„	10 33	...		—	12 15	2 30	5 7		6 27	—	7 57	9 57	—	—	...	—	—	—
63¾	Yarmouth (Vauxhall)	„	10 10	...		—	11 57	2 12	4 50		6 20	—	7 9	9 40	—	—	—	...	—	—
78¾	Ely	„	9 7	...		—		12 50	4 5		6 28	—			12 10	—	—	6 15	—	—
100¾	Cambridge	„	9 34	...		...		1 20	4 35		6 55	—	...	—	12 55	—	—	4 51	—	—
81¾	Peterborough	„	10 20	...		—	—	1 45	6 0		7 35	—	...	—	1 40	—	...	6 52	—	—
	Ipswich	„	...	—	11 53	—	—	...	...	4 16	6 26 / ...	—	—	8 36	—	—	—	—	—	—
167	**LONDON** St. Pancras	„	11 14	—	...	—	—	3 9 / 4 3	6 13	—	— / 8 35	—	...	—	—	—	—	—	—	—
	Lpool St.	„	11 10	...	2 10	—	...	2 58 / 4 0	6 8	6 0	8 15 / 8 30	—	—	...	3 10	—	...	7 0	—	—

¶ **Hethersett, Kimberley, Thuxton, Yaxham, North Elmham, and Ryburgh.**—The Trains although noted to call will stop only at these Stations when required to take up or set down Passengers. Passengers wishing to alight are requested to intimate the same to the Guard at the preceding stopping Station. Passengers wishing to be taken up should be at the Station Five Minutes before the time named in the Tables.
U Calls at Kimberley to take up Passengers for Norwich only. V Parliamentary from Stations between Wells and Kimberley inclusive to London and intermediate Stations. W Horses and Private Carriages are not conveyed by this Train for Stations between Wymondham and London.
● Will call when required to take up or set down Passengers. Passengers wishing to alight must intimate the same to the Guard at the preceding *stopping* Station.
Mixed Trains.—These Trains being Goods Trains with Passenger Carriages attached for the general convenience of the Public, the same punctuality cannot be observed as with ordinary Passenger Trains. ☞ Horses and Private Carriages are not conveyed by these Trains.

Public Timetables for the line, dated 1882.

NORWICH, DEREHAM, FAKENHAM, AND WELLS.

DOWN TRAINS. — WEEK DAYS / SUNDAYS.

Miles from Norwich	FROM		morn	morn	morn		morn	Parl. morn	morn	morn	morn	morn	even.	Mkt. even.	even.	even.	even	even.		Sun. Parl. even.			
	LONDON Lpool St.	dep.	—	5 10	6 10	Tuesdays only.	6 0	6 0	9 0	9 10	10 32	11 55	...	Saturdays only.	2 30	2 40	5 0	5 15	—	2 40	—	—	—
	St. Pancras		—	—	—		—	—	—	9 15	10 25	12 3	...		...	2 35	—	5 5	—	—	—	—	—
	Ipswich	dep.	—	7 8	7 8		...	—	11 20	...		...	—		4 35	...	6 45	—	—	—	—	—	—
	Peterborough	„	—	Via Forncett.	—		7 10	7 10	Via Forncett.	9 30		12 50	—		Via Forncett.	3 30	Via Forncett.	4 45	—	2 30	—	—	—
	Cambridge	„	—		—		8 30	8 26		10 45		1 23	...			4 17		5 40	—	4 58	—	—	—
	Ely	„	—		—		8 57	8 57		11 13		2 5	—			4 45		7 5	—	5 28	—	—	—
	Yarmouth (Vauxhall)	„	6 P 0		8 10		9 20	9 20		10 20		1 0	—	3 45		3 45		5 35	—	6 0	—	—	—
	Lowestoft	„	—		7 Q 12		8 47	8 47		10 5		12 40	—	3 30		3 30		6 18	—	—	—	—	—
	Cromer	„	...		6 30		8 50	8 50		10 10		12 30	...	3 30		3 30		6 33	—	—	—	—	—
	Norwich	dep.	7 0		8 50		10 20	10 30		12 46		3 10	...	4 45		5 55		8 0	—	7 0	—	—	—
1	Trowse		7 6		8 55		10 25	10 36		12 51		3 16	...	4 51		6 1	...	8 6	...	7 6	—	—	—
6¼	Hethersett		7 16	...	—		...	10 47				3 26		5 1		6 11	...	8 16	...	7 16	—	—	—
10¼	**Wymondham**	arr.	7 25	8 58	9 10		10 40	10 57	12 57	1 9		3 36		5 10	6 21	6 20	7 59	8 25	—	7 25	—	—	—
		dep.	7 27	8 59	9 11		10 41	10 59		1 12		3 40	Not on Saturdays.	5 12	6 25		8 0	8 28	...	7 28	—	—	—
14	Kimberley		7 34	—	—		—	11 7		1 20		3 48		5 20	6 33		...	8 36	...	7 36	—	—	—
16¼	Hardingham		7 39	9 10	9 21		10 52	11 14		1 26		3 53		5 25	6 38			8 41	...	7 41	—	—	—
17¾	Thuxton		7 43	—			...	11 18		..		3 57		5 29	6 42			8 46	—	7 46	—	—	—
19¾	Yaxham		7 49	—			●	11 24		R		4 2		5 35	6 49		...	8 52	—	7 52	—	—	—
21¼	**Dereham**	arr.	7 54	9 20	9 31		11 3	11 29		1 37		4 8		5 40	6 54		8 10	8 57	—	7 57	—	—	—
		dep.	7 57	Tuesdays only.	9 40		11 8	11 31		1 42		4 19	5 34	5 45	7 0		8 21	9 0	—	8 0	—	—	—
26	North Elmham		8 7		Runs to Lynn and Peterboro'.		Runs to Lynn.	11 41		1 52		4 29	5 44	5 56	7 10		8 32	9 11	—	8 11	—	—	—
31¼	Ryburgh		8 19					11 53		2 4		4 41	5 55	6 8	7 22		8 43	9 23	—	8 23	—	—	—
33¾	**Fakenham**		8 26					12 0		2 14		4 49	6 0	6 26	7 30		8 49	9 31	—	8 31	—	—	—
38¾	Walsingham		8 38					12 13		2 28		5 3		6 38	7 43		9 1	9 43	—	8 43	—	—	—
43¼	**Wells**	arr.	8 52					12 27		2 42		5 16	...	6 52	7 57		9 15	9 57	...	8 57	—	—	—

¶ **Hethersett, Kimberley, Thuxton, Yaxham, North Elmham, and Ryburgh.**—The Trains although noted to call will stop only at these Stations when required to take up or set down Passengers. Passengers wishing to alight are requested to intimate the same to the Guard at the preceding stopping Station. Passengers wishing to be taken up should be at the Station Five Minutes before the time named in the Tables.
P From Yarmouth on Mondays only.
Q From Lowestoft at 7.35 a.m. on Mondays. R Calls at Yaxham when required to set down Passengers.
Fakenham Market.—On Thursdays the Train leaving Fakenham for Wells at 4.49 p.m. will start at 5.0 p.m.
● Will call when required to take up or set down Passengers. Passengers wishing to alight must intimate the same to the Guard at the preceding *stopping* Station.
Mixed Trains.—These Trains being Goods Trains with Passenger Carriages attached for the general convenience of the Public, the same punctuality cannot be observed as with ordinary Passenger Trains.

operating authorities frowned on this practice, and GER working timetables dictated that Walsingham was not to be used as a crossing station.

Other developments in the last quarter of the 19th Century included the elimination of Barsham Tunnel and the provision of a south-to-west avoiding line at Dereham; the tunnel – which may have been cheaply-constructed with inadequate lining – was replaced by an open cutting with substantial retaining walls. Meanwhile at Dereham the continued growth of through traffic on the Norwich to Kings Lynn cross country route was resulting in considerable congestion and it seemed sensible, therefore to construct an avoiding line between Dereham South and Dereham West junctions, thereby reducing the amount of traffic needing to reverse in the passenger station. The new curve, which was opened in 1884, was designed primarily for freight traffic, and ordinary passenger services continued running into Dereham station on the old alignment.

An Unsuccessful Resort?

In general, development was rapid around a newly-opened seaside resort, and in some places the railway companies themselves took a lead in laying out streets and building guest houses; this happened for example at Hunstanton where the Lynn & Hunstanton Railway built an entire resort on a "green field" site. Elsewhere, speculative builders moved in to accelerate resort development and in this way Cromer was transformed from a fishing village to become one of the most fashionable watering places in East Anglia. (Significantly, Lord Suffield – a major landowner in the Comer area – was Chairman of the East Norfolk Railway Company.)

Curiously, such development did not occur at Wells, and while neighbouring Hunstanton and Cromer were enjoying unprecedented growth, the little port stubbornly refused to "develop" as a conventional resort. The reasons for this are complex, but not hard to find. In the Victorian period, seaside resorts were usually upper middle class residential towns, catering for permanent or long-stay patrons rather than day trippers. Typically, a Victorian or Edwardian businessman would purchase a villa or book rooms for use during the Summer, and at the start of the season his wife, children, nanny and servants would migrate *en masse* to the chosen resort. The head of the family might stay in London during the week and travel to the seaside at weekends, or (if there was a good train service) he could commute – and in this way the most popular resorts became long-distance commuter towns in their own right. The GER and other companies were only too glad to see this development taking place, and arranged prestige morning up and evening down expresses for their high class patrons. By 1910, the Great Eastern was providing restaurant car facilities to and from Clacton, Hunstanton, Cromer and its other top resorts, and such facilities did much to enhance the prestige of the resorts concerned.

Obviously, the price of property would increase in these successful resorts, and this, together with the actual cost of travelling, made long-distance commuting an expensive business. It followed that, if a Victorian family was going to take up residence by the sea, the heavy cost involved would have to be weighed against environmental and health factors, and resorts with attractive cliff scenery, dry sandy or gravel soils, mild climates and "healthy" air were preferred; an ideal resort for holidays or permanent residence might be from 50 to 100 miles from London, have cliff scenery and a health-giving climate. Sadly, Wells (a low-lying marshland town, 144½ miles from Liverpool Street) did not fulfil any of the above requirements, and it was not even *by* the sea – being about a mile away from the nearest beaches!

It seems that, as far as GER resorts were concerned, 140 miles was the *maximum* distance for long distance commuting, but an ideal distance was something under 100 miles from London. Only ultra rich and successful Victorian businessmen could afford to commute from places above 100 miles from London, but the resorts concerned tended to have above-average scenic attractions which made the long and expensive daily journey worthwhile (Cromer being the classic example). This point is underlined forcibly by the following table, which shows that Wells, *even if it had the requisite scenic attractions,* would have been further from London than any other GER resort town.

Table 2

DISTANCES FROM LIVERPOOL STREET OF GER SEASIDE RESORTS

Name of town	*Date of Rail Link*	*Distance (by usual route)*
Southend-on-Sea	1st October, 1889 (GER)	41½ miles
Southminster	1st June, 1889	45½ miles
Harwich	15th August, 1854	70¾ miles
Clacton-on-Sea	4th July, 1882	71 miles
Felixstowe Beach	1st May, 1877	85¾ miles
Aldburgh	12th April, 1860	99¼ miles
Hunstanton	3rd October, 1862	112¼ miles
Yarmouth	1st May, 1844*	128 miles
Mundesley-on-Sea	1st July, 1889	136¼ miles
Cromer	26th March, 1877	141¾ miles
Wells-next-the-Sea	1st December, 1857	144½ miles

* *Yarmouth not connected to London until 15th December, 1845.*

NORWICH, DEREHAM, FAKENHAM AND WELLS.

Junction with Cambridge Main Line at Wymondham.

Page	DOWN TRAINS.	Week Days morn	morn	morn	morn	morn	noon	S even.	even.	even.	even.	even.	even.	even.	even.	even.	even.	even.	Sundays even.
97	Yarmouth (Vaux.) ... dep.	...	7 33	...	9 15	...	12 0	12 53	3 15	3 15	...	3 40	5 5	...	6 5	...	7 23	...	6 0
97	Lowestoft — — — „	—	6 57	—	8 40	—	11§16	12 43	2 50	2 50	—	3 28	3 28	—	5 44	—	5E44	—	5 44
99	Cromer .... „	...	6B23	...	8 45	...	9 48	2 20	2 58	2 58	...	2 58	5 22	...	5 55	...	5 55	...	5 10
76 to 79	NORWICH (Thorpe) dep.	6 36	8 17	—	10 36	—	12 55	3 20	4 2	4 2	—	5 22	6 15	—	7 5	—	8 12	—	7 0
	Trowse	6 41	8 22	...	10 40	...	1 0	3 25	4 7	4 7	...	5 27	6 20	...	7 10	...	8 17	...	7 6
	Hethersett — — — — —	6 51	C	—	10 50	—	1 10	3 35	—	—	—	5 37	6 30	—	—	—	8 27	—	7 16
	Wymondham .... arr.	7 0	8 38	...	10 59	...	1 19	3 44	...	...	...	5 46	6 39	...	7 25	...	8 36	...	7 25
72-75 & 122	LONDON { Liverpool St. dep.	—	—	5 8	5 30	9 10	10 0	11 50	—	—	—	—	2 30	3 20	—	4 55	5 15	—	3 30
	LONDON { St. Pancras... „	...	...	...	...	9 15	...	12 5	...	...	...	...	2 35	...	...	...	5 5	...	...
122	Ipswich — — — — „	—	—	6 58	9 12	—	12 0	—	—	—	—		—	5 0	—	6 31	—	—	—
72-75	Cambridge .... „	...	6 45	Via Forncett.	8 5	10 50	...	1 30	...	...	...		4 6	...	...	...	6 40	...	5 0
91	Peterborough —dep.	—	—		7 10	9 25	Via Forncett	12 52	—	Saturdays only.	Tuesdays only. From Lynn.	Saturdays only.	3 30	Via Forncett	—	Via Forncett	4 53	7 7	4 40
82	YORK .... „	...	...		...	...		10 25	...				12 52		...		...	3 50	...
	Doncaster — — „	—	—		—	8 10		11 16	—				1 42		—		—	4 38	2 35
	Lincoln .... „	...	...		...	9 2		12 9	...				2 35		...		...	5 40	3 33
72-75	Ely — — — — — „	—	7 8		8 47	11 18		2 5	—				4 40		—		7 11	—	5 33
	Wymondham .... arr.	...	8 26	8 23	10 48	12 42	1 10	3 27	...			...	6 15	6 23	...	7 49	8 32	...	6 55
	Wymondham — — —dep.	7 3	8 40		11 1		1 21	3 49	—			5 47	6 44		7 27	7 51	8 39	Via Lynn.	7 28
	Kimberley	7 10	...		11 8		1 28	3 56	...			5 51	6 51		...	☛	8 47		7 36
	Hardingham — — — —	7 15	8 50		11 13		1 33	4 1	—	—		5 59	6 56		—		8 52		7 41
	Thuxton	7 19	☛		11 17		1 37	4 5	...	...		6 3	7 0		...	...	8 56		7 45
	Yaxham — — — — —	7 25			11 23		1 43	4 12	—	—	—	6 10	7 7		—	F	9 3		7 52
92	Dereham .... { arr.	7 30	8 59		11 28		1 48	4 17	4 38	4 38	5 46	6 15	7 12		7 44	8 8	9 8	9 15	7 57
	Dereham .... { dep.	7 33	9 7		11 31		1 53	4 23	4 41	4 43	5 50	6 18	7 16		7 49	8 11	9 20		8 0
	North Elmham — — —	7 42	9 16		11 40		2 2	4 32	To Lynn & Peterboro'.	4 53	5 59	6 27	7 25		To Lynn.	8 20	9 29		8 9
	County School	7 47	9 21		11 44		2 6	4 37		4 57	6 4	6 33	7 30			8 24	9 33		8 14
	Ryburgh — — — — —	7 54	9 28		11 51		2 13	4 44		5 4	6 11	6 40	7 37			8 31	9 40		8 21
	Fakenham	8 0	9 34		11 57		2 21	4S50		5 10	6 16	6 48	7 44			8 37	9 48		8 27
	Walsingham — — — —		9 45		12 8		2 32	5 1		5 21		7 0	7 54			8 47	9 58		8 38
95	WELLS .... arr.	...	9 58		12 22		2 45	5 15		5 34	—	7 15	8 8			9 0	10 10		8 52

Page	UP TRAINS.	Week Days morn		morn		morn		morn	morn	morn			even.	H even.		J even.		even.	even.		even.	even.	even.	Sundays even.
94	WELLS .... dep.	6 15	Mondays and Saturdays only.	7 15	Not on Mondays or Saturdays.	8 5		8 5	9X5	10 0		...	12 50	2 0		3 25		...	From Peterborough and Lynn.		5 58	7 15	...	5 0
	Walsingham — — — —	6 25		7 25		8 15		8 15	9X15	10 11		—	1 0	2 10		3 35		—			6 8	7 25	From Lynn.	5 11
	Fakenham........	6 35		7 35		8 25		8 25	9 38	10 21		...	1 10	2A32		3 46		5 10			6 18	7 35	...	5 22
	Ryburgh — — — — —	6 40		7 40		8 30		8 30	9 43	10 26		—	1 15	2 37		3 51		5 15			6 23		—	5 27
	County School........	6 47		7 47		8 38		8 38	9 50	10 33		...	1 22	2 44		3 58		5 22			6 30		...	5 34
	North Elmham — — —	6 53		7 53		8 43		8 43	9 55	10 39		—	1 27	2 48		4 3		5 28			6 37		—	5 41
93	Dereham .... { arr.	7 1		8 1		8 51		8 51	10 3	10 47		...	1 35	2 56		4 11		5 36	5 46		6 45		9 15	5 49
	Dereham .... { dep.	7 5		8 5		9 1		9 3	10 8	10 50		—	1 40	2 59		4 17	4 41		5 51		6 51		9 20	5 53
	Yaxham	7 10		8 10		...		Via Lynn.	10 13	10 55		...	1 45	...		4 22	Via Lynn.	...	...		6 56		...	5 58
	Thuxton — — — — —	7 16		8 16		—			10 19	11 1		—	1 51	—		4 28		—	☛		7 2		—	6 4
	Hardingham	7 20		8 20		9 11			10 23	11 5		...	1 55	...		4 32		Thursdays only.			7 7		...	6 9
	Kimberley — — — — —	7 25		8 25		—			10 28	11 10		—	2 0	—		4 37			—		7 12		—	6 14
	Wymondham .... arr.	7 31		8 31		9 20			10 34	11 16		...	2 6	3 15		4 43			6 7		7 18	Mondays and Wednesdays only. Will commence running 3rd June.	9 36	6 20
76-79	Wymondham — — —dep.	7T58		8 53		—	9 52	—	—	11 25	11 51	Not on Mons. or Sats.	2 33	3 17	—	5U5			—	6 53	7 38		10 53	6 37
	Ely .... arr.	9 7		10 34		...	Via Forncett	10 42	...	12 48	Via Forncett		4 3	Via Forncett	...	6 26			...	Via Forncett	9 4		13 13	7 41
80	Lincoln — — — „	11 6		—		—		12 17	—	2 22			8 5		—	9 59	8 5		—		—		—	—
	Doncaster .... „	11 59		...		...		1 12	...	3 28			9 0		...	11 0	9 0		...		...		...	...
	YORK — — — „	13 56		—		—		2 15	—	4 21			9 52		—	...	9 52		—		—		—	—
90	Peterborough...... „	10 5		11 50		...		11 22	...	1 46			5 59		...	7 36	6 42		...		...		1 43	...
76-79	Cambridge — — —arr.	9 35		11 5		—	—	11 14	—	1 21	—		4 34		—	6 55	—	—	—	--	9 35		12 45	8 11
122	Ipswich .... „	T		...		...	11 54	...	...	...	1 16		...	4 47	...	8 35	...	...	...	8 35	...		...	...
76-79 & 122	LONDON { St. Pancras „	11 17		1P50		—	--	1P50	—	2 50			6 15	—	—	8 40	—	—	—		—		—	9 45
	LONDON { Liverpool St. „	11†10		12 40		...	2 23	12 40	...	2 57	...		6 10	6 40	...	8 25	...	...	...	...	...		3 0	9 37
72 to 75	Wymondham — — —dep.	7 34		8 34		9 22	—	—	10 39	11 19	—	—	2 8	—	3 27	4 45	—	—	6 8	—	7 30		9 39	6 23
	Hethersett	7 42		8 43		...	...	...	10 48	11 27	...	...	2 16	...	3 36	4 54	...	...	L	...	7 29		...	6 32
	Trowse— — — — — —	7 52		8 51		9 37	—	—	10 59	11 37	—	—	2 26	—	3 46	5 4	—	—	6 23	—	7 39		9 54	6 42
	NORWICH (Thorpe) arr.	7 57		8 56		9 42	...	...	11 7	11 42	...	...	2 31	...	3 50	5 9	...	...	6 28	...	7 44		10 0	6 47
99	Cromer — — — —arr.	10 7		10 7		—	—	—	12 14	2 38	—	—	4K55	—	4 55	7 4	—	—	7 42	—	8 52	—	—	9 55
97	Lowestoft .... „	10 20		10 20		11§16	...	...	12 16	2 47	...	...	4M23	...	5 23	6 45	...	...	7 57	...	10 30	...	...	8 31
	Yarmouth (Vaux.) — „	8 54		10 13		10 42	—	—	12 8	1 10	—	—	4V52	—	4 52	6 15	—	—	7 13	—	8 55	—	10 50	8 24

NOTES.

A Arrives at Fakenham at 2.19 p.m.

B On Mondays leaves Cromer at 7.0 a.m.

C Calls at Hethersett on Tuesdays when required to take up Passengers.

E On Mondays, Thursdays, & Saturdays during June will leave Lowestoft at 7.0 p.m.

F Calls at Yaxham on Mondays when required to set down Passengers

H Passengers for Trowse, Norwich, Cromer, Yarmouth, and Lowestoft by this Train change at Wymondham.

J Horses and Private Carriages are not conveyed by this Train for Stations between Wymondham and London.

K On Thursdays during June will arrive at Cromer 3.43 p.m.

L Calls at Hethersett on Tuesdays when required to set down Passengers.

M On Saturdays due at Lowestoft 4.33 p.m.

N From Lowestoft on Saturdays only.

P During June will arrive at St. Pancras at 12.48 p.m.

S Fakenham Market.—On Thursdays this Train will leave Fakenham for Wells at 5.0 p.m.

T On Mondays only, Passengers for Ipswich and Liverpool St. leave Wymondham at 7.40 a.m., via Forncett, and arrive at Ipswich 9.3, and Liverpool Street at 10.45 a.m.

U On Saturdays leaves Wymondham at 5.22 p.m.

V On Thursdays during May will arrive at 3.26 p.m., commencing 1st June, will arrive at 3.26 p.m. every Week-day.

X From Wells and Walsingham on Saturdays only.

☛ Horses and Private Carriages not conveyed by these Trains.

§ To Lowestoft on Mondays, Thursdays and Saturdays only. Will commence running 1st June.

Public Timetable for May 1901.

NORWICH, DEREHAM, FAKENHAM AND WELLS.

Junction with Cambridge Main Line at Wymondham.

DOWN TRAINS. — WEEK DAYS / SUNDAYS

Reference to other Tables. PAGE	DOWN TRAINS.	morn	morn	morn	morn	morn	morn	noon	S even.	even.	even.	even.	even.	even.	even.	even.	even.	even.	even.	SUNDAYS even.
102	Yarmouth (Vaux.) ... dep.	...	7 33	...	...	9E8	...	12 0	12 57	3 15	3 15	...	3 40	5 8	...	6 5	...	7 22	...	6 0
	Lowestoft (Central) „	—	7 0	—	—	8 43	—	11N19	12 48	3 53	2 53	—	3 30	3 30	—	5 48	—	5 48	—	5 47
104	Cromer „	...	6 23	...	...	8Y45	...	10 0	2 25	2T58	2 54	...	2 54	5U20	...	5Z55	...	[illegible]55	...	5D10
78 to 82	NORWICH (Thorpe) dep.	6 36	8 17	—	—	10 35	—	12 55	3 20	4 2	4 2	—	5 22	6 17	—	7 5	—	8 12	—	7 0
	Trowse	6 41	8 22	...	...	10 40	...	1 0	3 25	4 7	4 7	...	5 27	6 22	...	...	...	8 17	...	7 6
	Hethersett	6 51	CC	—	—	10 50	—	1 10	3 35	—	—	—	5 37	6 32	—	—	—	8 27	—	7 16
	Wymondham arr.	7 0	8 38	...	...	10 59	...	1 19	3 44	...	...	...	5 46	6 41	...	7 23	...	8 36	...	7 25
74–77 & 132	LONDON { Liverpool St. dep.	—	—	5 5	5 23	—	9 10	10 0	12 0	—	—	—	—	3 35	3 20	—	4 55	5 12	—	3 30
	LONDON { St. Pancras „	...	...	...	...	...	9 15	...	12 20	...	...	...	...	3 40	...	...	...	5 5	...	...
132	Ipswich „	—	—	7 1	—	9 8	—	12 0	—	—	—	—	Saturdays only.	—	5 5	—	6 28	—	—	—
74–77	Cambridge „	...	6 45	...	8 15	...	10 52	...	1 37	...	...	...		4 6	...	...	...	6 36	R	5 0
94	Peterborough dep.	—	—	Via Forncett.	7 14	—	9 30	Via Forncett.	12 52	—	Saturdays only.	—		3 30	Via Forncett.	—	Via Forncett.	4 58	7 2	4 40
85	YORK „	...	...		...	...	...		10 25	...		Tuesdays only. From Lynn.		12 50		...		...	4 0	...
	Doncaster „	—	—		—	—	8 9		11 16	—				1 42		—		—	4 47	2 35
	Lincoln „	...	...		...	...	9 5		12 9	...				2 37		...		...	5 45	3 35
74–77	Ely „	—	7 8		8 47	--	11 18		3 6	—				4 37		—		7 9	—	5 33
	Wymondham arr.	...	8 25	8 25	10 16	10 48	12 37	1 10	3 27	...			...	6 15	6 32	...	7 47	8 20	...	6 58
	Wymondham dep.	7 3	8 40		11 1		1 21		3 49	—			5 47	6 46		7 25	7 49	8 39	Via Lynn.	7 28
	Kimberley	7 10	...		11 8		1 28		3 56	...			5 54	6 53		...	H	8 47		7 36
	Hardingham	7 15	8 50		11 13		1 33		4 1	—	—		5 59	6 58		—		8 52		7 41
	Thuxton	7 19	H		11 17		1 37		4 5	...	...		6 3	7 2		...		8 56		7 45
	Yaxham	7 25			11 23		1 43		4 12	—	—	—	6 10	7 8		—	F	9 3		7 52
95	Dereham { arr.	7 30	8 59		11 28		1 47		4 17	4 38	4 38	5 46	6 15	7 12		7 42	8 6	9 8	9 11	7 57
	Dereham { dep.	7 33	9 7		11 31		1 52		4 23	4 41	4 43	5 50	6 18	7 16		7 47	8 9	9 16		8 0
	North Elmham	7 42	9 16		11 40		2 0		4 32	To Lynn & Peterboro'.	4 52	5 59	6 27	7 25		To Lynn.	8 18	9 25		8 9
	County School	7 48	9 21		11 44		2 4		4 36		4 57	6 4	6 33	7 29			8 22	9 29		8 14
	Ryburgh	7 55	9 28		11 51		2 11		4 43		5 4	6 11	6 40	7 36			8 29	9 36		8 21
	Fakenham	8 0	9 34		11 57		2 19		4S49		5 10	6 16	6 48	7 42			8 35	9 42		8 27
	Walsingham		9 45		12 8		2 30		4 59		5 27		7 0	7 52			8 45	9 52		8 38
97	WELLS arr.	...	9 58		12 22		2 43		5 13		5 34	—	7 15	8 6			8 58	10 6		8 53

UP TRAINS. — WEEK DAYS / SUNDAYS

Reference to other Tables. PAGE	UP TRAINS.	Mondays only.	morn (Mondays only.)	morn (Not on Mondays.)	morn		morn	morn		morn		even.	G even.		J even.		even.	even.		even.	even.	SUNDAYS even.
98	WELLS dep.		6 15	7 15	8 5		8 5	9X5		10 0		12 50		1 58	3 25		...			5 58	...	5 0
	Walsingham		6 25	7 25	8 15		8 15	9X15		10 11		1 0		2 8	3 35		—	From Peterborough and Lynn.		6 8	From Lynn.	5 11
	Fakenham		6 35	7 35	8 25		8 25	9 38		10 21		1 10		2A30	3 46		5 10			6 18		5 22
	Ryburgh		6 40	7 40	8 30		8 30	9 43		10 26		1 15		2 35	3 51		5 15			6 23		5 27
	County School		6 47	7 47	8 38		8 38	9 50		10 33		1 22		2 42	3 58		5 22			6 30		5 34
	North Elmham		6 53	7 53	8 43		8 43	9 55		10 39		1 27		2 46	4 3		5 28			6 37	—	5 41
96	Dereham { arr.		7 1	8 1	8 51		8 51	10 3		10 47		1 35		2 54	4 11		5 36	5 46		6 45	9 11	5 49
	Dereham { dep.		7 4	8 4	9 1		9 3	10 8		10 50		1 40		2 57	4 17	4 41		5 51		6 51	9 16	5 53
	Yaxham		7 9	8 9	...		Via Lynn.	10 13		10 55		1 45		...	4 22	Via Lynn.	...	...		6 56	...	5 58
	Thuxton		7 15	8 15	—			10 19		11 1		1 51		—	4 28		—	H		7 2	R	6 4
	Hardingham		7 19	8 19	9 11			10 23		11 5		1 55		...	4 32		Thursdays only.			7 7	...	6 9
	Kimberley		7 24	8 24	—			10 28		11 10		2 0		—	4 37			—		7 12	—	6 14
	Wymondham arr.		7 30	8 30	9 20			10 34		11 16		2 6		3 13	4 43			6 7		7 18	9 32	6 20
74–82	Wymondham dep.	7 42	8 1	8 58	—	9 52	—	—	11 25	11 36	11 53	2 35	3 17	—	5W5			—	6 50	7 32	10 53	6 37
	Ely arr.	Mondays only.	9 6	10 34	...	Via Forncett.	10 42	...	...	12 48	Via Forncett.	4 2	Via Forncett.	...	6 26			...	Via Forncett.	8 58	12 13	7 41
83	Lincoln „		10 57	—	—		12 17	—	2 21	—		8 7		—	9 55	8 7		—		—	—	—
	Doncaster „		11 48	...	...		1 19	...	3 26	...		9 2		...	11 5	9 2		...		...	...	...
	YORK „		12 35	—	—		3 12	—	4 25	—		9 54		—	...	9 54		—		—	—	—
93	Peterborough „		10 5	11 44	...		11 22	..	1 45	...		5 52		...	7 28	6 41		...		...	1 43	...
78–82	Cambridge arr.		9 40	11 4	—	—	11 14	—	—	1 16	—	4 34	...	—	6 55	—	—	—	...	9 27	12 45	8 11
132	Ipswich „	9 4	—	...	...	11 54	...	...	...	...	1 16	...	4 47	...	8 35	...	...	...	8 35	...	...	...
78–82 & 132	LONDON { St. Pancras „	—	11 15	1 50	—	--	1 50	—	—	2 43		6 10	—	—	8 35	—	—	—		+	—	9 44
	LONDON { Liverpool St. „	10 45	11 10	12 40	...	2 35	12 40	...	...	2 49	...	6 6	6 40	...	8 26	...	...	...		...	3 0	9 37
74 to 77	Wymondham dep.	—	7 35	8 34	9 22	—	—	10 39		11 19		2 8	—	3 27	4 46	—	—	6 9	—	7 21	9 35	6 23
	Hethersett	...	7 43	8 42	B	...	...	10 48		11 27		2 16	...	3 36	4 54	...	...	L	...	7 29	...	6 32
	Trowse	—	7 52	8 51	9 37	—	—	10 59		11 37		2 26	—	3 46	5 4	—	—	6 24	—	7 39	9 50	6 42
	NORWICH (Thorpe) arr.	...	7 57	8 56	9 42	...	...	11 7		11 42		2 31	...	3 50	5 9	...	...	6 29	...	7 44	9 56	6 47
103	Cromer arr.	—	10 0	10 0	—	—	—	12 13		2 9		4 56	—	4 56	6 58	—	—	7 42	—	8 48	—	7 45
101	Lowestoft (Central) „	...	10P2	10P2	11K14	...	...	12 13		2 31		5M19	...	5 19	6 36	...	...	7 54	...	10 17	...	8 30
	Yarmouth (Vaux.) „	—	8 52	9 57	10 30	—	—	12 8		1 8		4V50	—	4 50	6 13	—	—	7 18	—	8 50	10 47	8 34

NOTES.

A Arrives at Fakenham at 2.17 p.m.

B Calls at Hethersett at 9.30 a.m. when required to take up Passengers.

CC Calls at Hethersett at 8.29 a.m. on Tuesdays when required to take up Passengers.

D During October will leave Cromer 5.45 p.m.

E Commencing 2nd November will leave Yarmouth at 9.15 a.m.

F Calls at Yaxham at 8.0 p.m. on Mondays when required to set down Passengers.

G Passengers for Trowse, Norwich, Cromer, Yarmouth, and Lowestoft by this Train change at Wymondham.

H Horses and Private Carriages not conveyed by these Trains.

J Horses and Private Carriages are not conveyed by this Train for Stations between Wymondham and London.

K To Lowestoft on Mondays only, and will run during October only.

L Calls at Hethersett at 6.16 p.m. on Tuesdays when required to set down Passengers.

M On Saturdays arrives at Lowestoft 4.32 p.m.

N From Lowestoft on Saturdays only.

P During October will arrive at Lowestoft 9.55 a.m.

R Calls at Thuxton at 9.23 p.m. when required to set down Passengers from March and Stations beyond.

S Fakenham Market.—On Thursdays this Train will leave Fakenham for Wells at 5.0 p.m.

T On Saturdays leaves Cromer at 2.54 p.m.

U On Saturdays leaves Cromer at 5.24 p.m.

V On Mondays, Thursdays, and Saturdays during October will arrive at 3.30 p.m.

W On Saturdays leaves Wymondham at 5.21 p.m.

X From Wells and Walsingham on Saturdays only.

Y During October will leave Cromer at 8.50 a.m.

Z On Saturdays leaves Cromer at 5.52 p.m.

Public Timetable for October 1908.

A further point which might be made with reference to the table is that Wells was one of the first East Anglian seaside towns to acquire a rail link – but this made no difference to its popularity (or lack of it) as a resort town.

Another factor which may have impeded resort development was the attitude of the Earl of Leicester – who as resident landlord could veto any plans put forward by outside developers. A paternalistic landlord of the old sort, Thomas Coke was probably interested in estate development rather than resort promotion, and one senses that this somewhat shy and retiring man would not have welcomed large scale resort development on his own doorstep. He was it seems happy to encourage the railway as a means of "improving" his beloved Holkham estate, and to this end he had actively promoted both the railway and the port of Wells; if, by building an embankment to enclose neighbouring marshland he also created an attractive "promenade", then so much the better. Townsfolk, farm tenants (perhaps even the occasional day trippers from Norwich) were welcome to visit the Earl's seaside lands, but when it came to building large hotels and laying out wide boulevards to encourage speculative building – in other words any kind of *large scale* development – the old Earl was less than enthusiastic. Furthermore, he was destined to live to a ripe old age (87) and in that long lifetime he never lost his firm, but benevolent grip on Holkham and Wells.

Locomotives and Train Services in GER Days

The original train service of four trains each way had increased to six up and six down workings by the end of the Century. Trains ran through from Norwich Thorpe to Wells, taking from 1 hour 40 minutes to 2 hours for the 43¼ mile trip, and there were additional trains between Norwich, Wymondham and Dereham, which continued (after reversal at the latter station) through to Kings Lynn. The West Norfolk branch was served by four trains each way between Heacham and Wells, but GER timetables did not encourage London travellers to use this route. Ironically, the distance from Liverpool Street to Wells via Heacham and the West Norfolk line was only 128¼ miles, and this compared very favourably with the 158½ miles via Norwich. However, the GER seemed reluctant to utilise the Heacham route to the full (perhaps because the busy Hunstanton branch could not have accommodated extra traffic between Heacham and Kings Lynn). Instead, the company made some small attempt to offer an improved service via Dereham and Wymondham – from where, on 2nd May, 1881, a "cut-off" had been opened between the Cambridge and Ipswich main lines; this cut-off shortened the distance between Wells and Liverpool Street to 144½ miles.

Diverging south eastwards from Wymondham, the "cut-off" line was double track throughout, with an intermediate station at Ashwellthorpe; it joined the Ipswich line some 32 chains north of Forncett station, thereby providing a short-cut for any future Wells to London through traffic. As we have seen, Wells-next-the-Sea did not attract Victorian holidaymakers – at least not in any appreciable quantity, and the new Forncett line was used mainly as a freight and diversionary route. Nevertheless, for travellers wishing to reach London in a hurry, the GER provided a 1.50 pm afternoon service from Wells, which missed out certain intermediate stops *en route* to Wymondham and terminated at Forncett at 3.08 pm. This provided a connection with the 2.55 pm express from Norwich Thorpe, allowing through travellers to reach London by 6.00 pm.

In the reverse direction it was possible, by leaving Liverpool Street on the 5.00 pm express and changing at Forncett, to be in Wells by 9.15 pm. The Forncett connections enabled through travellers to reach Wells in a little over four hours, but these times would clearly have been improved if trains had run non-stop to Wells. However, there was no point in running non-stop at a time in which so little traffic was offering itself; Wymondham, Dereham and Fakenham were, in any case, more important destinations and the Forncett connections were probably designed for Dereham travellers rather than for people making the through journey to Wells-next-the-Sea.

London travellers willing to study their timetables carefully might have found some reasonably-fast journey times via Heacham and the Hunstanton line, and although the infrequent services between Wells and Heacham may have forced many travellers to use the longer Forncett route, the West Norfolk line was a useful, though perhaps under-valued, alternative route to the capital. In 1909, for example, the 8.10 am from Wells to Heacham provided a 25 minute connection, giving travellers ample time to catch the 9.10 am express from Hunstanton to Liverpool Street. Overall time for the 128½ mile journey to London was 4½ hours and clearly, if the Great Eastern had wanted to run a fast through train between London and Wells the Heacham route would have offered many possibilities – although as pointed out above, such a service would not have served Dereham or other intermediate stops which were, in GER eyes, more important than Wells itself. (An added advantage of the Heacham route was the fact that through services were available from Hunstanton to St Pancras.)

Wells was served by three freight services, two of which ran via Dereham while the third travelled via Heacham and the West Norfolk branch. One of the Dereham workings started its journey at Norwich in the early hours of the morning, and returned from Wells at around

NORWICH, DEREHAM, AND WELLS BRANCH.

(Single Line between Dereham and Wells).

The Trains on the Single Line between Dereham and North Elmham are worked under the Electric Train Tablet System, in accordance with the Train Tablet Regulations (Tyer's Instrument No. 6). No Engine or Train is to be run on this Single Line without a Train Tablet. The Train Tablet Stations are Dereham and North Elmham.

The Trains on the Single Line between **North Elmham and Wells** *are worked by Train Staff and Train Staff Ticket, according to the "Train Staff Regulations" contained in the "Appendix" to this Working Time Book. No Engine or Train is to be run on this Single Line without a Train Staff or Train Staff Ticket. The Train Staff Stations are North Elmham, County School, Fakenham, Walsingham, and Wells.*

Down Trains—Week Days.

Miles from Norwich		FROM	1	2	3	4	5	6	7	8	9	10	11	12	13	14	15	16	17
				B Gds.	Pass.	Pass.	Eng.	◆ C Exp. Pass.	Pass.		D Gds.	Pass.	E Gds.	F Gds.	H Gds.	I Gds.	Pass.	Eng.	J Pass.
M.	C.			a.m.	a.m.	a.m.	a.m.	a.m.	a.m.		a.m.	a.m.	a.m.	a.m.	p.m.	p.m.	p.m.	p.m.	p.m.
		Beccles dep.	...	...	...	...	...	...	...	...	...	...	...	...	...	...	...	...	...
		Forncett "	...	...	...	...	...	...	...	...	...	...	...	...			...	...	...
		Yarmouth "	...	...	...	...	...	7 23	...	...	...	...	...	...			...	...	...
		Norwich (Thp.) dep.	...	4 30	6 10	...	7 45	8 17	...	...	...	10 35	10 40	10 40			12 55	...	3 30
1	0	Trowse arr.	...	4 37	6 13	...	...	8 21	...	...		10 39	10 45	10 45			12 59	...	3 34
		dep.	...	4 56	6 14	...	...	8 22	...	...		10 40	11 25	11 25			1 0	...	3 35
6	16	Hethersett "	...		6 24	...	...	C	...	...		10 50	...	...	...	...	1 10	...	3 38
10	18	Wymondham arr.	...	5 15	6 33	...	pass	8 37	...	...		10 59	11 50	11 50	...	...	1 19	...	3 44
		dep.	...	6 20	6 35	...	8 5	8 40	...	...		11 1	12 5	12 30	12 5	1 0	1 21	...	3 50
13	77	Kimberley "	...	B	6 42	...		...	...	...		11 8	E	1 10	H	...	1 28		3 57
15	60	Hardingham arr.	...	B	6 46	...		8 49	...	...		11 12	E	1 20	H	1 15	1 32		4 1
		dep.	...	...	6 47	...		8 50	...	...		11 13	...	1 50	...	1 50	1 33		4 2
17	10	Thuxton "	...	...	6 51			...	...	...	...	11 17	...	2 10	...	...	1 37		4 6
19	39	Yaxham "	...	B	6 57			...	...	...	...	11 23	E	2 30	H	...	1 43		4 12
21	51	Dereham arr.	...	7 15	7 2		8 12	8 59	...	...	...	11 28	1 10	2 40	12 50	2 10	1 47		4 17
		dep.	...	8 5	7 5			9 3	9 7	...	10 10	11 31	2 20	...	3 5	3 35	1 52		4 23
26	14	North Elmham arr.	...	8 17	7 13			...	9 15	...	10 22	11 39	...		3 17	3 47	1 59		4 31
		dep.	...	8 25	7 14			...	9 16	...	11 23	11 40			3 25	4 10	2 0		4 32
27	57	County School arr.	...	8 30	7 17				9 19	...	11 30	11 43			3 30		2 3		4 35
		dep.	...	8 45	7 18				9 21	...		11 44			3 40	4 17	2 4	3 30	4 36
31	31	Ryburgh "	...	9 5	7 25	...			9 28	...		11 51					2 11	...	4 43
33	62	Fakenham arr.	...	9 15	7 30	...			9 33	...		11 56					2 16	3 42	4 48
		dep.	...	10 25	...	7 36			9 34	...		11 57					2 19	...	4 49
38	58	Walsingham arr.	...	10 40	...	7 46			9 44	...		12 1					2 29		4 57
		dep.	...	10 50	...	7 47			9 45	...		12 3					2 30		4 58
		Wells T.P. arr.	...	...	...	8 0			9 56	...		12 20		...			2 41		5 10
43	21	Do. Station "	...	11 8	...	8 2		...	9 58	...		12 22		...			2 43		5 13
						Saturdays only.	Mons. & Thurs. only. To work 9.0 a.m. Up Train. Will not run after Monday, 8th September.	To Peterboro'. See page 85.			Not Saturdays. Eng. and Brk. from Nth. Elmham to County School.		Saturdays only. To King's Lynn. See page 87.	Not on Saturdays.	Not Saturdays. To Norwich. See page 115.	Saturdays only. To Norwich. See page 115.		Thursdays only. To work 5.5 p.m. Up Train.	

B No. 2. To shunt where required for No. 3 Passenger Train, and at Fakenham for No. 7 Passenger Train. To detach only at Kimberley, Hardingham, and Yaxham, and attach Traffic for Stations beyond Dereham, and to leave Brake Fish at those Stations when required.

C No. 6. May work from Norwich Hunting Horses for Dunham and Horses for Joint Line. On Tuesdays to call at Hethersett at 8.31 when required to take up Passengers.

D No. 9. To perform station shunting at North Elmham.

E No. 9. To call at Kimberley, Hardingham and Yaxham when required to leave Brake Goods and attach Traffic for King's Lynn and Stations beyond Dereham, and at Hardingham and Yaxham to detach Empty B.W's.

F No. 12. To shunt at Hardingham for No. 15 Passenger Train.

H No. 13. To call at Kimberley, Hardingham and Yaxham to attach traffic for Kings Lynn and Aylsham Line Stations and leave empty B.W's. To shunt at Dereham for No. 15 Passenger Train.

I No. 14. To shunt at Hardingham for No. 15 Passenger Train.

J No. 17. On Thursdays will leave Fakenham at 5.0 p.m. and be due Wells at 5.21 p.m.

No Down Goods or Ballast Train is to exceed 30 Loaded Trucks and the Break on leaving Walsingham for Wells.

WELLS HARBOUR BRANCH—*(Single Line).*

(Distance 69 Chains).

On Week Days the Engine of the 4.30 a.m. Goods Train from Norwich, and the Engine of the 4.50 p.m Goods Train from Wymondham, each makes a Trip between Wells Station and Wells Harbour.

Only one Engine in steam is to be allowed on the Wells Harbour Branch at one time.

NORWICH, DEREHAM, AND WELLS BRANCH.

(Single Line between Dereham and Wells.)

The Trains on the Single Line between **Dereham and North Elmham** *are worked under the Electric Train Tablet System, in accordance with the Train Tablet Regulations (Tyer's Instrument No. 6). No Engine or Train is to be run on this Single Line without a Train Tablet. The Train Tablet Stations are Dereham and North Elmham.*

The Trains on the Single Line between **North Elmham and Wells** *are worked by Train Staff and Train Staff Ticket, according to the "Train Staff Regulations" contained in the "Appendix" to this Working Time Book. No Engine or Train is to be run on this Single Line without a Train Staff or Train Staff Ticket. The Train Staff Stations are North Elmham, County School, Fakenham, Walsingham, and Wells.*

Down Trains—Week Days—*Continued.* / Sundays.

FROM	18	19	20	21	22	23	24	25	26	27	28	29	30	31	32	33 (Sundays)	34 (Sundays)
	Exp. Pass.	Pass.	Pass.	Pass.	B Gds.		D Pass.	E Pass.	F Exp. Cattle	◆ Pass.	I Pass.		J Exc.	K Pass.	Cars.	Pass.	Pass.
	p.m.	p.m.	p.m.	p.m.	p.m.		p.m.	p.m.	p.m.	p.m.	p.m.		p.m.	p.m.	p.m.	a.m.	p.m.
Beccles dep.	...	...	...	...	...	...	...	...	...	...	...	...		...	...	...	...
Forncett "	...	...	...	...	...	...	...	...	...	7 30	...	...	...	...	...	...	...
Yarmouth "	3 12	...	...	...	...	...	...	...	...	...	7 5	...	7 38	7 23	...	...	6 0
Norwich (Thp.) dep.	4 4	...	...	...	...	...	5 22	6 15	Class "A."	...	7 55	...		8 12	...	10 7	7 0
Trowse arr.	...		...	...	...	...	5 26	6 19	...	...	7 59	...	pass	8 16	...	10 11	7 5
dep.	...		...	...	...	...	5 27	6 20	6 40	...	8 0	...	8 10	8 17	...	10 12	7 6
Hethersett "	...		...		...	...	5 37	6 30	...	...		...		8 27	...	10 22	7 16
Wymondham arr.	pass		...		...	...	5 46	6 39	pass	7 49	8 15	...	pass	8 36	...	10 31	7 25
dep.	4 21		...		4 50	...	5 47	6 44	7 5	7 51	8 17	...	8 24	8 39	...	10 33	7 28
Kimberley "	...		...		B	...	5 54	6 51	...	...	...	...		8 47	...	10 40	7 36
Hardingham arr.	...		...		B	...	5 58	6 55	F	...	...	...		8 51	...	10 44	7 40
dep.	...		...		...	...	5 59	6 56	...	...	...	...		8 52	...	10 45	7 41
Thuxton "	...		...		B	...	6 3	7 0	...	...	...	...		8 56	...	10 49	7 45
Yaxham "	...		...		B	...	6 10	7 6	F	...	...	...		9 3	...	10 55	7 52
Dereham arr.	4 33	...	...	...	5 50	...	6 15	7 10	7 40	8 8	8 34	...	8 39	9 8	...	11 0	7 57
dep.	4 41	4 43	5 5	5 58	7 25	...	6 18	7 14	...	8 11	8 41	...	8 41	9 18	9 30	11 3	8 8
North Elmham arr.	...	4 51	5 13	6 3	B	...	6 26	7 22		8 19	...	...		9 26		11 11	8 16
dep.		4 52	5 14	6 4	7 45	...	6 27	7 23		8 20	...	...		9 27	9 39	11 12	8 17
County School arr.		4 56	5 18	6 8	B	...	6 31	7 27		8 23		...		9 30		11 16	8 21
dep.		4 57	5 19	6 9	7 53	...	6 32	7 29		8 24		...		9 31	9 44	11 17	8 23
Ryburgh "		5 4	...	6 16	8 15	...	6 40	7 35		8 31		...		9 38	...	11 24	8 29
Fakenham arr.		5 9		6 21	8 25	...	6 46	7 40		8 36		...		9 43		11 29	8 34
dep.		5 10		...	8 55	...	6 48	7 42		8 37		...		9 44	9 57	11 30	8 35
Walsingham arr.		5 20		...	9 10	...	6 58	7 51		8 46		...		9 53		11 40	8 45
dep.		5 21		...	9 20	...	7 0	7 52		8 47		...		9 54	10 11	11 41	8 46
Wells T.P. arr.		5 32		...	...	...	7 12	8 4	...	8 56		...		10 6	...	11 53	8 58
Do. Station "		5 34		...	9 40	...	7 15	8 6	...	9 0		...		10 8	10 22	11 55	9 0
	To King's Lynn, March, & Peterboro'. See page 87.	Saturdays only.	To Foulsham. See page 115.	Tuesdays only.			Saturdays only.		Saturdays only.	See page 192.	To King's Lynn. See page 88.		Mons. & Thur. only. To King's Lynn. See page 88. Will not run after Monday, 8th Sept.		Mons. Weds., and Sats.		

B No. 22. To call at Kimberley, Hardingham, Thuxton, and Yaxham, if required, to detach only. To call at North Elmham when required to detach traffic or attach Cattle and leave Brake Goods, and at County School to leave or take in Brake Goods. To shunt Dereham for Nos. 24 and 25 and at Fakenham for No. 27 Passenger Trains.

D No. 24. Runs to King's Lynn, via Heacham. See No. 12 Up, page 96. No. 24 may work from Norwich not exceeding 4 Trucks of Cattle for West Norfolk Line Stations, if the Trucks are fitted with Westinghouse Brake pipes. To cross No. 32 Up Passenger Train at County School.

E No. 25. On Tuesdays may work 1 Truck of Cattle only from Dereham for either Walsingham or Fakenham, if the Truck is fitted with Westinghouse Brake pipes.

F No. 26. Engine and Brake will leave Norwich for Trowse at 5.50 p.m. To call at Hardingham and Yaxham if required to detach Cattle only. To be extended as required. Dereham to arrange. Engine, &c., to return to Norwich as a Special.

I No. 28. Passengers for Stations King's Lynn side of Dereham on Mondays and Thursdays *until 8th September*. are to change at Dereham into No. 30 Train.

J No. 30. *Runs via Wensum Curve.*

K No. 31. May work Cattle from Wymondham for Dereham or Fakenham, if the Trucks are fitted with Westinghouse Brake pipes, but Trucks for both Stations must not be attached at one time.

No Down Goods or Ballast Train is to exceed 30 Loaded Trucks and the Brake on leaving Walsingham for Wells.

Part of the Working Timetable for July 1913.

11.00 am. Meanwhile, a second train had left Beccles, and, travelling via Forncett and Wymondham, it reached Wells in the early afternoon. The West Norfolk freight left Kings Lynn at 10.47 am, and arrived at Heacham by 12.25. Gaining the West Norfolk branch this third train then pursued its leisurely course through the north Norfolk countryside, reaching Wells in the early afternoon.

The Wells branch was worked for many years by the famous "No.1 Class" or "Little Sharpie" 2–4–0s, the first five of which had been delivered to the GER in 1867. Built by Neilson Reid & Co., they had originally been designed for the North British Railway, but the type was so successful in GE service that three further engines were built at Stratford, and these became the prototypes of the "No.1 Class", of which forty were constructed between 1867 and 1872. Thirty of the new engines were constructed by Sharp Stewart & Co., and a further ten were built at Stratford. They had 5ft 7in. driving wheels and 16 in. x 22 in. inside cylinders.

When new, the "No. 1 Class" locomotives were painted in a dark green livery with brown underframes, but in the 1880s (by which time paint technology had increased the range of paints available to Victorian railway companies) Great Eastern engines started to appear in the attractive Royal Blue livery that became the GER's trademark. Many of the "No. 1 Class" had by then been rebuilt with characteristic Holden boilers and, with their tall stove pipe chimneys and smart blue livery, they were attractive little engines, well-suited to light branch line duties.

In 1902, Wells-based "Little Sharpie" No. 117 became a local celebrity when it was elaborately decorated to mark the coronation of King Edward VII. Driver Woodhouse and Fireman Houseago decided to show their patriotism by adorning their engine with flags, drapes, garlands, flowers and ornaments, and though the end result might have been (to modern eyes) rather excessive, No. 117 worked a normal diagram on Coronation Day, becoming the centre of attraction at every station between Wells and Norwich!

Edwardian Wells

Having stagnated for over half-a-century, Wells appeared quaint and picturesque even in the Edwardian era, and G.W. Potter, arriving by train in about 1909, noted that the station was "on a very small scale throughout" in relation to "modern day stock". Writing in the *Railway Magazine* he gave an interesting description of the town as it appeared at that time:

> Although the town is called Wells-next-the-Sea to distinguish it from Wells in Somerset, it is a considerable distance from the sea, and except by a

> stretch of the imagination can hardly be termed a seaside resort. The tiny station lies inland; and when one has traversed the narrow and quaint little streets of the town and descended to the broad quay with its lines of railway, at which the boats are loading or unloading, only the first part of the journey to the shore has been accomplished. Speaking generally, the quay here runs east and west, but at its western termination the creek turns straight out to sea in a northerly direction. By its side is a high earthen rampart, forming a very pleasant promenade, and furnished with seats. On the one hand a view is obtained eastwards in the direction of Blakeney, and on the other are seen low-lying pasture lands intersected by broad water channels, bounded on the seaward side by a long line of dark green firs and pines. A lifeboat house stands at the junction of land and sea, and refreshment rooms are provided in a sheltered nook. Otherwise one looks back to the distant town of Wells-next-the-Sea, and lazily makes conjectures about the length of the promenade, the distance the crew would be compelled to travel should their services be required to man the lifeboat, and the genius who first gave the more or less appropriate title of Wells-next-the-Sea to this quaint little Norfolk seaport town.

Other writers echoed these thoughts, the general impression being that Wells was a quaint old seaport with few formal attractions. This was not necessarily a condemnation, and if Wells did not attract conventional Edwardian holidaymakers it had already gained favour with lovers of the quiet and the picturesque; in the longer term, Wells *did* have a future as a holiday resort, and it had clearly been "discovered" by the end of the 19th Century. In the meantime, the GER had done very little to encourage an influx of tourists, and the Wells branch in 1900 was not very different from the Wells branch of 1857.

The somnolent pace of local life was rudely shattered on 26th August, 1912, when (not for the last time) Norfolk was paralysed by severe flooding. On that memorable day, 6 inches of rainfall fell in a period of 12 hours and the normally-tranquil River Stiffkey was transformed into a raging torrent which washed away part of the embankment at East Barsham and destroyed bridge No. 1724 at nearby North Barsham; a freight train had been crossing the bridge when it collapsed, but fortunately the bulk of the train reached safety before the failure occurred. Meanwhile, the Norwich to Ipswich main line had been obstructed at Flordon, and in the next few days Norwich to London trains were diverted via Forncett and Wymondham – reversing at the latter place in order to continue their journeys.

World War One

On 4th August, 1914 the German army marched into Belgium, and at midnight Britain declared war; the ensuing conflict cost 1,114,789 British lives and brought to an end the halcyon Edwardian era in which railways had played a central role in society and the economy.

NORWICH, DEREHAM AND WELLS.

Single Line between Dereham and Wells.

Miles from Norwich.	DOWN WEEK DAYS.		1	2	3	4	5	6	7	8	9	10	11	12	13	14
				Engs.		Eng.	Pass.	Gds.	Pass.	Pass.	Pass.	Eng.	Pass.	Pass.	Pass.	Gds.
	See page									127						
																NS
				a.m.		a.m.	a.m.	a.m.	a.m.	a.m.	a.m.	a.m.	a.m.	a.m.	p.m.	p.m.
	Forncett	dep.														
	Yarmouth	"	—	—	—	—	—	—	—	7 27	—	—	—	—	—	—
	Norwich (Thorpe)	arr.								8 6						
		dep.	—	—	—	—	—	4 30	6 37	8 11	—	—	—	10 33	—	—
1 0	Trowse	arr.						4 37								
		dep.	—	—	—	—	—	4 50	—	—	—	—	—	—	—	—
6 16	Hethersett	"							6 52	8 26				10 48		
10 18	Wymondham	arr.		—	—		—	5 15	7 0	8 34	—	—	—	10 56	—	—
		dep.						6 20	7 3	8 37				10 59		12 5
13 77	Kimberley	"	—	—	—	—	—	**	7 10	8 44	—	—	—	11 6	—	**
15 60	Hardingham	arr.						**	7 14	8 48				11 10		**
		dep.	—	—	—	—	—	—	7 15	8 49	—	—	—	11 11	—	—
17 10	Thuxton	"							7 20	8 53				11 15		
19 59	Yaxham	"	—	—	—	—	—	**	7 28	8 59	—	—	—	11 21	—	**
21 51	Dereham (T)	arr.						7 15	7 31	9 4				11 28		12 51
		dep.	—	4 20	—	5 47	7 3	7 50	7 37	9 7	9 20	9 38	9 50	11 35	12 16	
26 14	North Elmham (T)	arr.					7 10	8 2	7 44		9 27		9 57	11 42	12 23	
	(See note) (S)	dep.	—	4 29	—	5 56	7 11	8 12	7 45	—	9 28	9 47	9 58	11 43	12 24	—
27 57	County School (S)	arr.					7 15	8 18	7 49		9 32	9 50	10 2	11 47	12 28	
		dep.	—	4 33	—	6 0	7 18	8 50	7 50	—	9 33	10 13	10 11	11 48	12 30	—
31 21	Ryburgh							9 10	7 57		9 40			11 55		
33 62	Fakenham (S)	arr.	—	—	—	6 12	—	9 20	8 2	—	9 45	—	—	12 0	—	
		dep.		4 45		6 16		10 35	8 4		9 47	10 23		12 2		
38 58	Walsingham (S)	arr.	—	—	—	—	—	10 50	8 14	—	9 57	—	—	12 12	—	—
	(See note)	dep.		4 55		6 26		11 0	8 15		9 58	10 35		12 13		
43 21	Wells (S)	arr.	—	5 5	—	6 36	—	11 15	8 25	—	10 8	10 45	—	12 23	—	—
		dep.														
	To			For 5.40 & 5.55 a.m. ex Wells.		7.8 a.m. ex Wells.	Norwich.			Peterboro'.		For 11.18 a.m. ex Wells.	Norwich.		Norwich.	
	See page						134			107			134		134	

Miles from Norwich.	DOWN WEEK DAYS.		15	16	17	18	19	20	21	22	23	24	25	26	27	28
			Gds.	Gds.	Gds.	Pass.	Pass.	Pass.	Gds.	Gds.	Pass.	Pass.	Cars.			Pass.
	See page							221								
			SO	NS	SO				NThS	ThO			ThO			
			a.m.	a.m.	p.m.	p.m.	p.m.	p.m.	p.m.	p.m.	p.m.	p.m.	p.m.			p.m.
	Forncett	dep.														
	Yarmouth	"	—	—	—	—	—	—	—	—	2 25	—	—	—	—	—
	Norwich (Thorpe)	arr.									3 8					
		dep.	10 30	10 30	—	1 0	—	—	—	—	3 17	—	3 50	—	—	—
1 0	Trowse	arr.	10 35	10 35												
		dep.	11 6	11 6	—	—	—	—	—	—	—	—	—	—	—	—
6 16	Hethersett	"				1 15					3 32					
10 18	Wymondham	arr.	11 25	11 25	—	1 23	—	—	—	—	3 40	—	pass	—	—	—
		dep.	12 5	12 40	12 45	1 25					3 44		4 5			
13 77	Kimberley	"	**	1 0	—	1 32	—	—	—	—	3 51	—	—	—	—	—
15 60	Hardingham	arr.	**	1 10	1 0	1 36					3 55					
		dep.	—	1 42	1 15	1 37	—	—	—	—	3 56	—	—	—	—	—
17 10	Thuxton	"		2 16		1 41					4 0					
19 59	Yaxham	"	**	2 36	—	1 47	—	—	—	—	4 6	—	—	—	—	—
21 51	Dereham (T)	arr.	1 10	2 46	1 35	1 52					4 11					
		dep.	2 44		2 55	2 2	1 56	2 17	2 55	3 2	4 20	4 18	4 27	—	—	4 42
26 14	North Elmham (T)	arr.			**		2 3	2 24	**	**		4 25				4 49
	(See note) (S)	dep.	—	—	3 12	—	2 4	2 25	3 12	3 19	—	4 26	4 34	—	—	4 50
27 57	County School (S)	arr.					2 9	2 29				4 30				4 54
		dep.	—	—	3 17	—	2 10	2 32	3 17	3 24	—	4 31	4 40	—	—	4 55
31 21	Ryburgh						2 17					4 38				
33 62	Fakenham (S)	arr.	—	—	—	—	2 22	—	—	—	—	4 43	4 52	—	—	—
		dep.					2 24					4 44				
38 58	Walsingham (S)	arr.	—	—	—	—	2 34	—	—	—	—	4 54	—	—	—	—
	(See note)	dep.					2 35					4 55				
43 21	Wells (S)	arr.	—	—	—	—	2 45	—	—	—	—	5 5	—	—	—	—
		dep.														
	To		King's Lynn.		Norwich.	March, Ely & Liverpool St.		Norwich.	Norwich.	Norwich.	York.		For 5.0 p.m. up train.			Norwich.
	See page		107		134	107		134	134	134	107					134

6 To shunt at Dereham for 7, and at Fakenham for 8 and 9. Calls at Kimberley, Hardingham and Yaxham, to detach only and attach traffic for stations beyond Dereham, and to leave brake fish at those stations when required.
14 Calls at Kimberley, Hardingham and Yaxham to attach traffic for King's Lynn and Aylsham line stations and leave empty B.W.'s.
15 To call at Kimberley, Hardingham and Yaxham when required to leave brake goods and attach traffic for King's Lynn and stations beyond Dereham, and at Hardingham and Yaxham to detach empty B.W.'s.

16 Due to arr. Kimberley 12.50 and Thuxton 1.47. To shunt at Hardingham for 18.
17 To call at North Elmham when required for brake goods for East Norfolk line only.
21 & 22 To call at North Elmham, when required, for brake goods for East Norfolk line only.
Nth. Elmham.—A passr. train must not be arranged to cross another passr. train at this station.
Walsingham.—Trains must not be arranged to cross at this station. No down goods or ballast train is to exceed 20 loaded trucks and the brake on leaving Walsingham for Wells.

On this and the next three pages are shown the Working Timetables of the lines for January 1917.

NORWICH, DEREHAM AND WELLS.

Single Line between Dereham and Wells.

DOWN WEEK DAYS.

		29	30	31	32	33	34	35	36	37	38	39	40	41	42	43	44	45	46	47	48	49	50	51
				Gds.	Pass.	Eng.			Pass.		Pass.		Pass.											
See page									128															
					SO	NS																		
				p.m.	p.m.	p.m.			p.m.		p.m.		p.m.											
Forncett	dep																							
Yarmouth	"	—	—	—	—		—	—	5 3	—	—	—	—	—	—	—	—	—	—	—	—	—	—	—
Norwich (Thorpe)	arr.								5 47															
	dep.	—	—	—	5 20	—	—	—	6 5	—	—	—	9 0	—	—	—	—	—	—	—	—	—	—	—
Trowse	arr.																							
	dep.	—	—	—	—	—	—	—	—	—	—	—	—	—	—	—	—	—	—	—	—	—	—	—
Hethersett	"								6 20				9 13											
Wymondham	arr.	—	—	—	5 38	—	—	—	6 28	—	—	—	9 21	—	—	—	—	—	—	—	—	—	—	—
	dep.			*5 5*	5 40	*5 40*			6 30				9 27											
Kimberley	"	—	—	**	5 47	—	—	—	6 37	—	—	—	9 34	—	—	—	—	—	—	—	—	—	—	—
Hardingham	arr.	—	—	**	5 51	—	—	—	6 41	—	—	—	9 38	—	—	—	—	—	—	—	—	—	—	—
	dep.	—	—	—	5 52	—	—	—	6 42	—	—	—	9 39	—	—	—	—	—	—	—	—	—	—	—
Thuxton	"	—	—	**	5 56	—	—	—	6 46	—	—	—	9 43	—	—	—	—	—	—	—	—	—	—	—
Yaxham	"	—	—	**	6 2	—	—	—	6 52	—	—	—	9 49	—	—	—	—	—	—	—	—	—	—	—
Dereham (T)	arr.			*6 0*	6 7	*6 10*			6 57				9 54											
	dep.	—	—	*7 20*	6 9	—	—	—	7 2	—	8 24	—	9 58	—	—	—	—	—	—	—	—	—	—	—
North Elmham (T)	arr.			*7 42*	6 16				7 9		8 31		10 5											
(see note) (S)	dep.	—	—	*7 49*	6 17	—	—	—	7 10	—	8 32	—	10 6	—	—	—	—	—	—	—	—	—	—	—
County School (S)	arr.			**	6 21				7 14		8 36		10 10											
	dep.	—	—	*7 57*	6 22	—	—	—	7 15	—	8 38	—	10 11	—	—	—	—	—	—	—	—	—	—	—
Ryburgh	"			*8 15*	6 29				7 22				10 18											
Fakenham (S)	arr.	—	—	*8 25*	6 34	—	—	—	7 27	—	—	—	10 23	—	—	—	—	—	—	—	—	—	—	—
	dep.			*9 10*	6 35				7 28				10 24											
Walsingham (S)	arr.	—	—	*9 25*	6 45	—	—	—	7 38	—	—	—	10 34	—	—	—	—	—	—	—	—	—	—	—
(see note)	dep.			*9 35*	6 46				7 39				10 35											
Wells (S)	arr.	—	—	*9 55*	6 56	—	—	—	7 49	—	—	—	10 45	—	—	—	—	—	—	—	—	—	—	—
	dep.				7 18																			
To					King's Lynn.	(For 7.25 p.m. up goods.)					Norwich.													
See page					119						134													

SUNDAYS.

		1	2	3	4	5
		Eng.		Pass.		
See page				129		
		p.m.		p.m.		
Forncett	dep			6 0	—	—
Yarmouth	"					
Norwich (Thorpe)	arr.			6 52		
	dep.	—	—	7 0	—	—
Trowse	arr.					
	dep.	—	—	—	—	—
Hethersett	"			7 16		
Wymondham	arr.	—	—	7 25	—	—
	dep.			7 28		
Kimberley	"	—	—	7 36	—	
Hardingham	arr.			7 40		
	dep.	—	—	7 41	—	
Thuxton	"			7 45		
Yaxham	"	—	—	7 52	—	—
Dereham (T)	arr.			7 57		
	dep.	*3 30*	—	8 0	—	—
North Elmham (T)	arr.			8 8		
(see note) (S)	dep.	*3 39*	—	8 9	—	—
County School (S)	arr.			8 13		
	dep.	*3 43*	—	8 14	—	—
Ryburgh	"			8 21		
Fakenham (S)	arr.	—	—	8 26	—	—
	dep.	*3 55*		8 27		
Walsingham (S)	arr.	—	—	8 37	—	—
(see note)	dep.	*4*		8 38		
Wells (S)	arr.	*4 15*	—	8 52	—	—
	dep.					
To		For 4.45 p.m. ex Wells.				
See page						

31 To call at Kimberley, Hardingham, Thuxton and Yaxham, if required; to detach only, and at County School to leave or take in brake goods. To shunt at Dereham for 36, and on Saturdays where required for 32.

— **32** May work from Norwich not exceeding 4 trucks of cattle for West Norfolk line stations, if the trucks are fitted with Westinghouse brake pipes.

— **40** May work cattle from Wymondham for Dereham or Fakenham, if the trucks are fitted with W'house brake pipes, but trucks for both stations must not be attached at one time.

North Elmham.—A pass. train must not be arranged to cross another pass. train at this station.

Walsingham.—Trains must not be arranged to cross at this station. No down goods or ballast train is to exceed 20 loaded trucks and the brake on leaving Walsingham for Wells. Down road traffic for Coleman's Sdg. to be detached at Walsingham, & worked back 1.40 & 3.30 p.m. ex Wells.

WELLS, DEREHAM AND NORWICH.

Single Line between Wells and Dereham.

UP WEEK DAYS.		1	2	3	4	5	6	7	8	9	10	11	12	13	14	15	16	17	18	19	20	21	22	23	24	25	26
		Pass.	Eng.			Gds.	Pass.	Pass.		Pass.	Pass.		Gds.	Gds.	Pass.	Eng.	Pass.	Gds.	Pass.	Pass.	Exp. Catle. Gds.	Pass.	Eng.	Eng.			Gds.
From						5.15 a.m. ex King's Lynn.	7.0 a.m. ex Norwich.			9.30 a.m. ex Norwich.	10.18 a.m. ex King's Lynn.		5.50 a.m. ex Norwich.	5.50 a.m. ex Norwich.			11.50 a.m. ex Norwich.			2.22 p.m. ex Norwich.	Class B.		12.30 p.m. ex Dereham.	For 7.0 Dereham to Norwich.			
See page						106	134			134	106		134	134			134			134							
						SO					SO		NS	SO							SO		SO	SO			NS
		a.m.	a.m.			a.m.	a.m.	a.m.		a.m.	a.m.		a.m.	a.m.	a.m.	p.m.	p.m.	a.m.	p.m.	p.m.	p.m.	p.m.	p.m.	p.m.			p.m.
Wells (S)	dep.	5 55						9 25							10 48			11 18	12 50		2 48	3 17		4 40			
Walsingham (S)	arr.	6 4	—	—	—	—	—	9 34	—	—	—	—	—	—	10 57	—	—	11 33	12 59	—	3 3	3 26	—	4 51	—	—	—
(see note)	dep.	6 5						9 35							10 58			11 43	1 0		3 38	3 27		4 57			
Fakenham (S)	arr.	6 14	—	—	—	—	—	9 44	—	—	—	—	—	—	11 7	—	—	11 58	1 9	—	3 53	3 36	—		—	—	—
	dep.	6 15						9 50							11 8			1 17	1 11		4 0	3 37		5 9			
Ryburgh	"	6 20	—	—	—	—	—	9 55	—	—	—	—	—	—	11 13	—	—	1 40	1 16	—	4 18	3 42	—	—	—	—	—
County School (S)	arr.	6 26					8 21	10 1		10 48			11 10	11 10	11 19		1 5		1 22	3 36	4 28	3 48					
	dep.	6 27	—	—	—	—	8 23	10 3	—	10 50	—	—	11 28	11 28	11 20	—	1 7	1 50	1 23	3 37	4 57	3 49	—	5 22	—	—	—
North Elmham (S)	arr.	6 31					8 27	10 7		10 54			11 33	11 33	11 24		1 11	1 55	1 27	3 41	5 2	3 53					
(see note) (T)	dep.	6 32	—	—	—	—	8 28	10 8	—	10 55	—	—	12 0	11 55	11 25	—	1 12	2 26	1 28	3 42	5 15	3 54	—	5 28	—	—	—
Dereham (T)	arr.	6 40				6 50	8 36	10 16		11 3	pass		12 14	12 10	11 33		1 20	2 38	1 36	3 50	5 27	4 2		5 36			
	dep.	6 42	7 0	—	—	7 40	—	10 22	—	—	11 11	—	—	—	11 40	12 30	—	3 20	1 40	—	5 42	4 14	—	—	—	—	4 45
Yaxham	"	6 47				* *		10 27							11 45			* *	1 45			4 19					5 0
Thuxton	"	6 53	—	—	—	—	—	10 33	—	—	—	—	—	—	11 51	—	—	—	1 51	—	—	4 25	—	—	—	—	5 30
Hardingham	arr.	6 56				8 5		10 36							11 54			* *	1 54			4 28					5 40
	dep.	6 57	—	—	—	8 25	—	10 37	—	—	—	—	—	—	11 55	—	—	—	1 55	—	—	4 29	—	—	—	—	6 5
Kimberley	"	7 2						10 42							12 0			* *	2 0			4 34					6 40
Wymondham	arr.	7 8	7 30	—	—	pass	—	10 48	—	—	pass	—	—	—	12 6	12 55	—	4 0	2 6	—	6 7	4 40	—	—	—	—	6 55
	dep.	7 10				8 40		10 51			11 28				12 8				2 9		6 35	4 42	4 46				7 25
Hethersett	"	7 19	—	—	—	—	—	11 0	—	—	—	—	—	—	12 17	—	—	—	2 18	—	—	4 51	—	—	—	—	—
Trowse	arr.					9 5															7 0						7 50
	dep.	—	—	—	—	9 15	—	—	—	—	—	—	—	—	—	—	—	—	—	—	7 20	—	—	—	—	—	8 10
Norwich (Thorpe)	arr.	7 31				9 20		11 15			11 44				12 29				2 30		7 25	5 3	5 8				8 15
	dep.	—	—	—	—	—	—	—	—	—	—	—	—	—	—	—	—	—	—	—	—	—	—	—	—	—	—
Yarmouth	arr.																										
Forncett	"	—	—	—	—	—	—	—	—	—	—	—	—	—	—	—	—	—	—	—	—	—	—	—	—	—	—
See page																				148							

Walsingham.—Trains must not be arranged to cross at this station.

North Elmham.—A passenger train must not be arranged to cross another passenger train at this station.

5 Calls at Yaxham to detach traffic or attach cattle for Trowse.

— 7 On Wednesdays may work 1 truck cattle (2 on Fridays and Sats.) from Fakenham to Norwich, if truck is fitted with Westinghouse brake pipes. The Yarmouth and Aslé traffic to go forward from Norwich by goods train.

— 10 Runs via Dereham South Curve. **12 and 13** To shunt at County School for 14.

15 On Sats. to perform yard shunting at Wymondham, leaving there for Norwich 4.46 p.m.

17 To shunt at Fakenham for 18. Calls at Yaxham and Hardingham if required to detach or attach cattle and traffic for stations on E.U. Line or W.V. branch. On Sats. calls at Kimberley if required to attach traffic for stations on E.U. Line and W.V. Branch.

20 To call at Coleman's Siding (between Walsingham and Fakenham) when required. To shunt at Walsingham for 21. London cattle worked by this train between Wells and Dereham to be brought into Dereham next engine. To call at County School when required to leave brake goods.

— 21 Will not convey horses and private carriages for stations between Wymondham and London.

23 To run to Dereham attached to 19.

26 To shunt at Wymondham for 34, and on Thursdays where required for 27.

WELLS, DEREHAM AND NORWICH.

Single Line between Wells and Dereham.

UP WEEK DAYS.		27	28	29	30	31	32	33	34	35	36	37	38	39	40	41	42	43	44	45	46	47	48
		Pass.	Pass.			Gds.	Gds.	Gds.	Pass.	Pass.		Gds.		Gds.	Pass.	Pass.	Eng.	Pass.			Eng.		
From			4.20 p.m. ex Norwich.							3.35 p.m. ex Peterboro'.						7.0 p.m. ex Peterboro'.	E. of 6.13 pm ex Heacham & 6.5 p.m. ex Norwich.	8.28 p.m. ex Norwich.			E. of 5.5 p.m. ex Wymondham and 9.0 ex Norwich.		
See page			134							106						106		134					
		Th O				S O	NThS	Th O				T O		N S									
		p.m.	p.m.			p.m.	p.m.	p.m.	p.m.	p.m.		p.m.		p.m.	p.m.	p.m.	p.m.	p.m.			p.m.		
Wells (S)	dep.						3 30	3 30	5 43						8 35		8 45				11 10		
Walsingham (S)	arr.	—	—	—	—	—	3 45	3 45	5 52	—	—	—	—	—	8 44	—	—	—	—	—	—	—	—
(see note)	dep.						3 55	3 55	5 54						8 45		8 56				11 20		
Fakenham (S)	arr.	—	—	—	—	—	4 25	4 25	6 3	—	—	—	—	—	8 54	—	—	—	—	—	—	—	—
	dep.	5 0					4 55	5 0	6 6						8 55		9 7				11 30		
Ryburgh	"	5 5	—	—	—	—	5 20	5 25	6 13	—	—	—	—	—	9 0	—	—	—	—	—	—	—	—
County School (S)	arr.	5 11	5 35				* *	* *	6 19						9 6		9 21	9 42					
	dep.	5 12	5 36	—	—	—	5 45	5 45	6 21	—	—	—	—	—	9 7	—	—	9 43	—	—	11 42	—	—
North Elmham (S)	arr.	5 16	5 40				5 50	5 50	6 25						9 11			9 47					
(see note) (T)	dep.	5 17	5 41	—	—	—	6 5	6 5	6 30	—	—	—	—	—	9 12	—	—	9 48	—	—	11 46	—	—
Dereham (T)	arr.	5 25	5 49				6 20	6 20	6 38	6 35					9 20	9 34		9 56			11 55		
	dep.	5 26	—	—	—	7 0	7 55	7 30	—	6 43	—	7 15	—	7 25	—	9 39	—	—	—	—	—	—	—
Yaxham	"					*	*	7 41		6 48													
Thuxton	"	—	—	—	—	*	*	*	—	6 58	—	—	—	—	—	—	—	—	—	—	—	—	—
Hardingham	arr.					7 30	*	8 6		7 1				* *		9 48							
	dep.	—	—	—	—	7 52	—	8 10	—	7 3	—	—	—	—	—	—	—	—	—	—	—	—	—
Kimberley	"					*	*	8 35		7 9													
Wymondham	arr.	5 43	—	—	—	8 30	8 40	8 45	—	7 15	—	7 55	—	9 0	—	9 59	—	—	—	—	—	—	—
	dep.	5 44				10 5	9 15	9 15		7 18		8 10		10 5		10 1							
Hethersett	"	—	—	—	—	—	—	—	—	7 27	—	—	—	—	—	—	—	—	—	—	—	—	—
Trowse	arr.					10 30	9 40	9 40				9 55		10 30									
	dep.	—	—	—	—	10 40	9 55	9 55	—	—	—		—	10 45	—	—	—	—	—	—	—	—	—
Norwich (Thorpe)	arr.	6 0				11 5	10 0	10 0		7 36				11 5		10 17							
	dep.		—	—	—	—	—	—	—	7 43	—	—	—	—	—	—	—	—	—	—	—	—	—
Yarmouth	arr.									8 32													
Forncett	"	—	—	—	—	—	—	—	—	—	—	—	—	—	—	—	—	—	—	—	—	—	—
See page										125													

SUNDAYS.		49	50	51	52	53	54
			Pass.		Eng.		
From					Eng. of 7.0 p.m. ex Norwich.		
			p.m.		p.m.		
Wells	dep.		4 45		9 10		
Walsingham	arr.	—	4 54	—	—	—	—
	dep.		4 56		9 20		
Fakenham	arr.	—	5 4	—	—	—	—
	dep.		5 8		9 30		
Ryburgh	"	—	5 16	—	—	—	—
County School	arr.		5 22				
	dep.	—	5 25	—	9 42	—	—
North Elmham	arr.		5 29				
	dep.	—	5 34	—	9 46	—	—
Dereham	arr.		5 42		9 55		
	dep.	—	5 46	—	—	—	—
Yaxham	"		5 53				
Thuxton	"	—	5 59	—	—	—	—
Hardingham	arr.		6 3				
	dep.	—	6 5	—	—	—	—
Kimberley	"		6 11				
Wymondham	arr.	—	6 17	—	—	—	—
	dep.		6 23				
Hethersett	"	—	6 32	—	—	—	—
Trowse	arr.						
	dep.	—	—	—	—	—	—
Norwich (Thorpe)	arr.		6 47				
	dep.	—	—	—	—	—	—
Yarmouth	arr.						
Forncett	"	—	—	—	—	—	—
See page							

31 Class B. To shunt at Wymondham for 41. Runs into and of Crown Point sidings.
32 To call at Coleman's siding (between Walsingham and Fakenham) when required and shunt at Dereham for 35. To call at County School when required for brake goods.
33 To call at Coleman's siding (between Walsingham and Fakenham) when required and shunt at Dereham for 35. To call at County School when required for brake goods.
=34 On Saturdays to cross at County School 34 down, leaving there 6.23 p.m., and run 2 minutes later to Norwich. Due to arrive Yaxham 6.47, Thuxton 6.54, and Kimberley 7.7 p.m.
39 To work from Dereham important N.C. traffic and tranships, also Trowse cattle off 3.30 p.m. ex Wells. To call at Hardingham, if required, for London and N.C. traffic, meat and market goods, that station to advise Dereham what they have to go on. Dereham to arrange and advise guard and driver. To shunt at Wymondham for 32, 33 & 41. Engine to perform shunting at Wymondham. To run into and out of Crown Point siding.
42 To run from County School to Dereham attached to 42.
−50 Due to arrive Ryburgh 5.13, Yaxham 5.50, and Kimberley 6.9 p.m.

North Elmham.—A passenger train must not be arranged to cross another passenger train at this station.
Walsingham.—Trains must not be arranged to cross at this station.

Conventional military thinking envisaged that any sudden German attack would take place in East Anglia, and for this reason north Norfolk was heavily-garrisoned throughout World War I. There were fears of a German naval attack, and indeed on 25th April, 1916 an enemy squadron ineffectively shelled Lowestoft. In the event the main threat to East Anglia came, not from the sea but from the air, and from 1915 until 1918 enemy Zeppelins flew across Norfolk more or less at will. The first raid occurred on 19th January, 1915 when the airship L4 dropped bombs near Hunstanton and on Kings Lynn; thereafter the raids took place with considerable frequency, and despite improved ground defences and a nightly "blackout" Dereham was bombed by a Zeppelin raider in 1915.

In the days before effective road transport, railways were expected to play a vital role in the British defensive system – and in the event of an invasion lines such as the Wells branch would have been used to transport men, horses and equipment to threatened coastal areas. A concomitant of this vital defensive function was the appearance of rail-mounted guns and mobile armoured trains – one of the latter being stationed in north Norfolk. Built by the London & North Western Railway at Crewe this curious assembly consisted of a Great Northern 0–6–2T marshalled between two bogie infantry wagons and two gun-carrying vehicles. The whole train was encased in steel plate, and it could be driven either from the locomotive or from push-pull type control positions at each end of the gun wagons; for offensive armament the train was equipped with naval-type 12 pounders and rapid-firing maxim machine guns. Based on the M& GN at North Walsham the armoured train could be rushed to any threatened part of the coast, and it was frequently seen on patrol on coastal lines such as the West Norfolk branch.

In general the war resulted in a gradual reduction in services, but the Wells branch retained a relatively "full" train service throughout the war. One adverse result of the 4-year conflict was the abandonment of the Great Eastern's royal blue livery; in its place engines were painted in a drab dark grey and the pre-war colour scheme was never revived.

Local railways remained in a state of readiness until the early months of 1918, but as the war approached its end the anti-invasion precautions were scaled-down; by August, it was clear that Germany was on the point of defeat. The Zeppelin raids nevertheless continued almost to the bitter end, and on 5th August, 1918 the "monster" airship L70 appeared over north Norfolk. On this occasion the Germans were unlucky, and a British aeroplane managed to destroy the raider; mortally wounded, L70 fell into the sea off Wells, and in the next few days hundreds of people thronged local beaches hoping to see the wreck. The destruction of L70 was, for local people, a fitting conclusion to the Great War, which ended with an Armistice in the following November.

The Last Days of the GER

The bitter struggle against Imperial Germany had left all railways in a run-down condition, and recovery was not helped by a coal strike in 1920/21. In spite of these problems, the Wells branch was still served by seven trains each way. The January 1921 timetable provided four morning and three afternoon workings between Wells and Norwich, balanced by three morning and four afternoon services in the opposite direction. Additional short distance workings ran between Wells and Dereham on Saturdays only, while the cross country service between Norwich and Kings Lynn provided many extra workings on the southern part of the branch. The post-war freight service was similar to that in operation before 1914, with minor variations in arrival and departure times. The West Norfolk branch was served by four trains each way, with good connections for London available at Heacham; most West Norfolk services still terminated at Heacham, but one or two workings continued through to Hunstanton after reversal. (In 1921 the 10.12 am and 12.55 pm departures from Wells both worked through, but in later years only the later train served Hunstanton directly.)

Locomotives seen at Wells in the early 1920s were mainly 'T26' or "Intermediate" 2–4–0s, which had replaced the long-serving "No. 1 Class" engines just before World War I. The 'T26s' were superficially similar to the rebuilt "No. 1 Class" – but of considerably greater dimensions; they had 5ft 8in. coupled wheels and 17½ in. x 24 in. inside cylinders. Goods services were often worked by Worsdell 'Y14' class 0–6–0s – the standard GER mixed traffic type. Larger engines were rarely used, and most Norwich–Wells and West Norfolk branch services were handled by these two familiar Great Eastern locomotive classes. All passenger trains were, in 1921, still formed of archaic short-wheelbase stock.

Before leaving the Great Eastern period, it would be fitting to make at least some mention of that company's fascinating multi-coloured ticket system. Briefly, tickets issued at Wells and other GER stations were coloured in accordance with a directional colour code. In the up direction, the relevant colours were yellow, blue and buff for 1st, 2nd and 3rd class bookings respectively; the corresponding "down" colours were white, red and green. Tickets for through bookings to St Pancras were further distinguished by horizontal coloured stripes (a 3rd class single from Wells to St Pancras, for example, would have

NORWICH, WYMONDHAM, DEREHAM, FAKENHAM AND WELLS.

Down — WEEK-DAYS.

See page / Station	morn	morn	morn	morn	morn	morn	morn	morn
(35 to 37) LONDON (Liverpool St.) dep						5 8		5 50
Cambridge „						6 39		8 12
Ely „						7 7		8 49
Wymondham arr.						8 29		10 12
(30) LONDON (Liverpool St.) dep						5 0		
Ipswich „						6 56		
Forncett „						8 20		
Wymondham arr.						8 33		
(38 to 40) NORWICH (Thorpe) dep		6 17			7 52	8 20		
Trowse „		6 22			7 57			
Hethersett „		6 33				8 34		
Wymondham arr.		6 41			8 13	8 42		
Wymondham dep.		6 44			8 15	8 44		
Kimberley „		6 51			8 22	E		
Hardingham „		6 56			8 27	8 55		
Thuxton „		7 1			8 31			
Yaxham „		7 7			8 38			
Dereham arr.		7 12			8 46	9 5		
Dereham dep.	6 45	7 18	7 22	8 30	8 51	9 9	9 10	
North Elmham „	6 53	7 27		8 38		9 17		
County School „	6 57	7 32		8 42		9 22		
Ryburgh „		7 40				9 29		
Fakenham „		7D56				9 37		
Walsingham „		8 7				9 48		
WELLS arr.		8 20				10 1		
	To Wroxham.		To King's Lynn.	To Wroxham.	To King's Lynn.		To King's Lynn.	

Station	morn	morn	even	morn	even	morn	NS even	NS even
LONDON (Liverpool St.) dep						11 50		
Cambridge „	9SO10			10 6		1 24		
Ely „	9SO33			10 43		1 53		
Wymondham arr.	10SO38			12 1		3 7		
LONDON (Liverpool St.) dep				10 0				
Ipswich „	9 0			11 57				
Forncett „	10 28			1 1				
Wymondham arr.	10 41			1 14				
NORWICH (Thorpe) dep	10 35			12 59		3 9		
Trowse „	10 40			1 4		3 14		
Hethersett „	10 51			1 15		3 25		
Wymondham arr.	11 0			1 23		3 34		
Wymondham dep.	11 3			1 25		3 38		
Kimberley „	11 10			1 32		3 46		
Hardingham „	11 15			1 37		3 52		
Thuxton „	11 19			1 41		3 57		
Yaxham „	11 25			1 47		4 4		
Dereham arr.	11 30			1 52		4 9		
Dereham dep.	11 35	11 43	12 10	1 56	1 57	4 17	4 18	4 47
North Elmham „	11 43		12 18	2 4			4 26	4 55
County School „	11 48		12 22	2 10			4 33	4 59
Ryburgh „	11 55			2 17			4 40	
Fakenham „	12 2			2 24			4 46	
Walsingham „	12 13			2 35			4 57	
WELLS arr.	12 26			2 48			5 10	
		To King's Lynn.	To Wroxham.		To King's Lynn.	To King's Lynn.		To Wroxham.

Station	SO even	SO even	even	even	even	even	MC even	SUNDAYS even
LONDON (Liverpool St.) dep								3 25
Cambridge „				4 15				5 0
Ely „	2 15			5 0				5 45
Wymondham arr.	3 39			6 24				7 9
LONDON (Liverpool St.) dep	12 25			3 15		5 22		
Ipswich „	2 14			5 0		7 0		
Forncett „	3 48			6 22		8 5		
Wymondham arr.	4 1			6 37		8 18		
NORWICH (Thorpe) dep	3 54			6 22		7 39		6 59
Trowse „				6 27		7 44		
Hethersett „				6 38		7 55		7 16
Wymondham arr.	4 13			6 46		8 3		7 25
Wymondham dep.	4 15			6 49		8 20		7 30
Kimberley „				6 56		8 27		7 38
Hardingham „	4 25			7 2		8 32		7 43
Thuxton „	4 29			7 6		8 36		7 47
Yaxham „				7 12		8 42		7 54
Dereham arr.	4 38			7 17		8 47		7 59
Dereham dep.	4 41	4 53	7 7	7 21	7 23		8 51	8 2
North Elmham „	4 49		7 18	7 29			8 59	8 11
County School „	4 54		7 22	7 34			9 4	8 16
Ryburgh „	5 2			7 41			9 11	8 23
Fakenham „	5 8			7 47			9 18	8 29
Walsingham „	5 19			7 59			9 29	8 40
WELLS arr.	5 32			8 12			9 42	8 53
		To King's Lynn.	To Wroxham.		To King's Lynn.			

Up — WEEK-DAYS.

See page / Station	MO morn	NM morn	MO morn	NM morn	morn	morn	morn	morn
					From Wroxham.	From King's Lynn.		From King's Lynn.
WELLS dep	5 55						7 30	
Walsingham „	6 5						7 40	
Fakenham „	6 15						7 51	
Ryburgh „	6 20						7 58	
County School „	6 27				7 39		8 6	
North Elmham „	6 32				7 44		8 11	
Dereham arr.	6 40				7 52	8 18	8 19	10 4
Dereham dep.	6 42	6 42	7 8	7 25			8 23	
Yaxham „	6 47	6 47					8 28	
Thuxton „	6 53	6 53					8 34	
Hardingham „	6 57	6 57	7 18	7 35			8 38	
Kimberley „	7 2	7 2					8 43	
(35 to 37) Wymondham arr.	7 10	7 10	7 29	7 46			8 51	
Wymondham dep.	7 12	7 12					8 54	
Hethersett „	7 21	7 21					9 3	
Trowse „	7 29	7 29					9 11	
NORWICH (Thorpe) arr.	7 34	7 34					9 16	
(30) Wymondham dep.	7 30	7 53	7 30	7 53			9 10	
Forncett arr.	7 43	8 6	7 43	8 6			9 23	
Ipswich „	8 51	10 20	8 51	10 20			12 14	
LONDON (Liverpool St.) „	10 39		10 39					
(38 to 40) Wymondham dep.	7 52	7 52	7 52	7 52			9 9	
Ely arr	9 23	9 23	9 23	9 23			10 26	
Cambridge „	9 56	9 56	9 56	9 56			11 4	
LONDON (Liverpool St.) „		11 27		11 27			12 37	

Station	morn	morn	SO morn	even	even	even	even	even
		From Wroxham.	From King's Lynn.	From King's Lynn.		From Wroxham.		From King's Lynn.
WELLS dep	9 15				12 50		3 17	
Walsingham „	9 25				1 0		3 27	
Fakenham „	9 40				1 10		3 37	
Ryburgh „	9 45				1 15		3 42	
County School „	9 52	11 1			1 22	3 26	3 49	
North Elmham „	9 59	11 6			1 27	3 31	3 54	
Dereham arr.	10 7	11 14	11 12	1 17	1 35	3 39	4 2	4 5
Dereham dep.	10 13		11 20		1 38		4 11	
Yaxham „	10 18		11 25		1 43		4 16	
Thuxton „	10 24		11 31		1 49		4 22	
Hardingham „	10 29		11 35		1 53		4 26	
Kimberley „	10 34		11 40		1 58		4 31	
Wymondham arr.	10 42				2 6		4 39	
Wymondham dep.	10 47				2 9		4 42	
Hethersett „	10 56				2 18		4 51	
Trowse „	11 5				2 28		4 59	
NORWICH (Thorpe) arr.	11 10		12 4		2 33		5 4	
Wymondham dep.	12 22				3 16		4 50	4A42
Forncett arr.	12 35				3 31		5 3	
Ipswich „	2 58		2A55		4 43		6SO25	7A49
LONDON (Liverpool St.) „			4A55					
Wymondham dep.	10 54				2 18		4 47	
Ely arr	12 19				3 18		6 13	
Cambridge „	12 52				3 47		7 1	
LONDON (Liverpool St.) „	2 21				5 17		8 33	

Station	even (Thursdays only.)	even	even	even	even	even	SUNDAYS even
		From Wroxham.	From King's Lynn.		From King's Lynn.	From Wroxham.	
WELLS dep				5 40			4 40
Walsingham „				5 51			4 51
Fakenham „	4 20			6 3			5 3
Ryburgh „	4 25			6 10			5 11
County School „	4 32	6 7		6 18		9 49	5 20
North Elmham „	4 37	6 12		6 27		9 54	5 29
Dereham arr.	4 45	6 20	6 34	6 35	9 47	10 2	5 37
Dereham dep.	4 48			6 42	9 52		5 41
Yaxham „				6 48			5 48
Thuxton „				6 57	B		5 54
Hardingham „	4 58			7 2			6 0
Kimberley „				7 8			6 6
Wymondham arr.	5 9			7 16	10 16		6 14
Wymondham dep.	5 10			7 19	10 19		6 20
Hethersett „				7 28			6 29
Trowse „	5 24			7 36	10 33		
NORWICH (Thorpe) arr.	5 29			7 41	10 38		6 44
Wymondham dep.	5A50						
Forncett arr.							
Ipswich „	7A49						
LONDON (Liverpool St.) „							
Wymondham dep.	5 21			8 6	10 51		6 28
Ely arr	6 28			9 34	12 13		7 40
Cambridge „	7 1			10 4	12 45		8 14
LONDON (Liverpool St.) „	8 33				2 50 morn		9 40

A Via Norwich.
B Calls at Thuxton 10.1 p.m. when required to set down passengers only.

D Arrives Fakenham at 7.45 a.m.
E On Mondays calls at Kimberley 8.50 a.m. when required to set down passengers only.

MO Mondays only.
NM Not Mondays.
NS Not Saturdays.

SO Saturdays only.
TO Tuesdays only.
X Via Trowse.

For service between Dereham and King's Lynn, see page 56. For service between County School and Wroxham, see page 63.

Passenger Timetable for 3rd October, 1921.

been buff with a broad blue stripe). In later years this system was simplified; GER 2nd class tickets were abolished (outside London) in 1893, and directional colours were abandoned in 1914 – thereafter 1st and 3rd class tickets became plain white and plain buff respectively.

In 1923 the independent life of the Great Eastern Railway came to an end, for the Government had decided (as an alternative to nationalisation) that the main line railway companies would be grouped into four main regional organisations; the necessary Act of Parliament was passed in 1921 and a few months later the Wells branch became part of the London & North Eastern Railway.

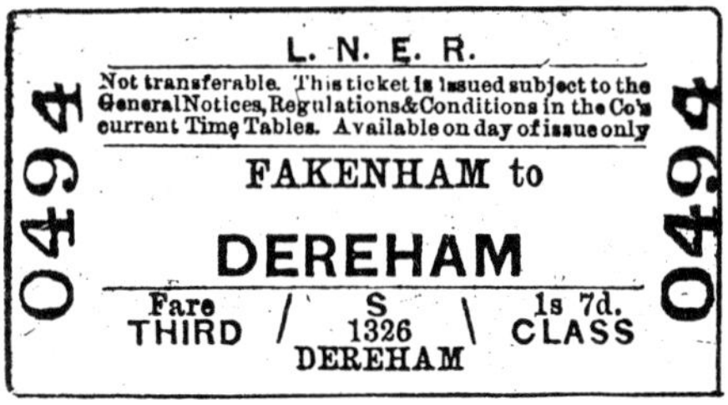

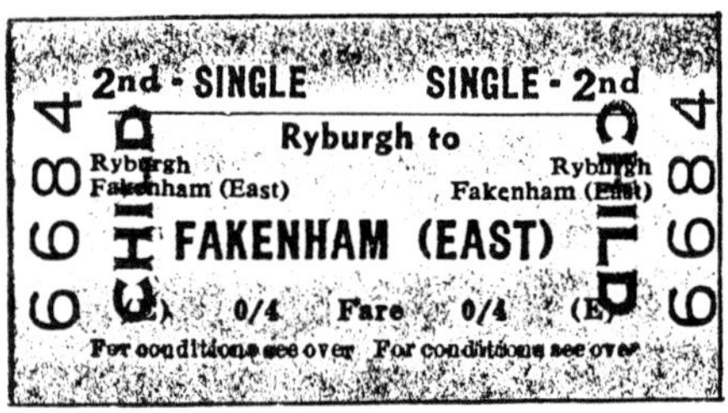

Chapter Four

The LNER Period (1923–1947)

The London & North Eastern Railway was the poorest of the "Big Four" main line companies created at the Grouping, and although in 1908 the Great Eastern, Great Central and Great Northern companies had contemplated a voluntary merger, many East Anglians felt a pang of regret when the once-proud Great Eastern became part of such a ramshackle amalgamation. The LNER lavished money on new locomotives and rolling stock for its prestigious East Coast Main Line, but the branch lines of East Anglia did not benefit from this new investment, and much of the former GE system was obliged to struggle on with elderly Victorian equipment that should, perhaps, have been renewed before World War I. This was particularly unfortunate as far as the Wells branch was concerned, for this remote and very rural route had been starved of investment even in the Great Eastern period.

Locomotives and Rolling Stock in the LNER Period

In Edwardian days the Wells branch trains, with their blue locomotives and smart teak coaches, had made an attractive sight in the rolling landscape of north Norfolk; after 1923 they were, arguably, slightly less pleasing to the eye. Coaches had been painted crimson red during the last years of Great Eastern ownership, but this livery was replaced in the LNER period by a drab overall brown mixture that was sometimes called "teak brown". However, it was extremely difficult to remove the red paint from former GER coaches, and the "teak" was in most cases brown paint; true varnished teak (either real or "scrumbled") was confined to new or main line vehicles.

The coaches used on local services during the 1920s were exclusively 6-wheelers, but bogie vehicles appeared once a week in the form of a Tuesday-only through portion from Liverpool Street. Bogie coaches were used in greater numbers during the 1930s, though older short wheelbase stock was still used on school services and for "strengthening" purposes. An innovation, at this time, was the introduction of an LNER steam railcar on certain offpeak services – there was for example a Thursday-only market day trip from Dereham to Fakenham.

Locomotives seen on the branch in the 1920s and 1930s included former GER 'T26' 2–4–0s, which became (in the LNER's rationalised classification system) 'E4' 2–4–0s. The 'E4s' worked both Norwich–Wells and Wells–Heacham services, becoming, in many ways the "classic" Wells branch locomotive type. Another class seen in the LNER period were the familiar Worsdell 0–6–0 mixed traffic engines, which became the LNER's 'J15' class; these locomotives worked both passenger and goods services. Other ex-GER 0–6–0s, including 'J17s' and (to a lesser extent) 'J19s' appeared in increasing numbers throughout the 1930s. Claud Hamilton 4–4–0s appeared sporadically in the years before World War II, and by the later 1930s it was possible to see 'D15s', 'D16/2s' and 'D16/3s' at work on the branch.

Another class of ex-GER 4–4–0s used in the 1930s were the former 'T19' rebuilds, which became 'D13s' under the LNER classification system; these were probably the first "large" locomotives seen at Wells, and their appearance caused considerable excitement among youthful "spotters"! The Tuesday-Only through coaches from London were hauled, not by 4–4–0s but by 'F3' 2–4–2Ts, and towards the end of the 1930s former Great Northern Railway 'D2' 4–4–0s were introduced into the area. These "foreigners" undoubtedly added an element of variety to an otherwise exclusively Great Eastern scene, but local train crews seem to have preferred their "own" engines, claiming that the Ivatt engines were unsuitable for service on the heavily-graded Wells line.

Passenger and Freight Services

The train service provided by the LNER was little different to that offered in the Great Eastern era, and there were still only half a dozen workings each way; the March 1938 timetable, for instance, showed five up and six down workings, with various additional services on Mondays and Saturdays. On Sundays, there was just one train each way, departing from Wells at 4.50 pm and returning from Norwich at 7.09 pm. The through Forncett service no longer ran from Wells – though it was still possible in the 1930s to make use of this "short cut" to London by changing at Dereham. The Dereham to Wymondham portion of the line (which was of course shared by Norwich–Wells and Norwich–Kings Lynn trains) was served by about ten workings each way – including some steam railcar trips.

Freight services included two up and two down workings between Wymondham and Wells, together with one working from Kings Lynn to Wells via the West Norfolk branch. The Beccles working no longer ran, having been replaced by separate Beccles–Wymondham and Wymondham–Wells services.

Freight carried on the line was mainly coal or fertiliser inwards and agricultural products outwards, and goods rolling stock used on the branch reflected this range of traffic. In earlier years open wagons had predominated, and a typical Norwich to Wells freight train might have included GER 7-plank coal wagons, 5-plank general merchandise vehicles and 10-ton ventilated vans. Agricultural machinery was brought into the area on flat "engine wagons" while fish traffic from Wells was conveyed in the Great Eastern's special fish vehicles. An unusual source of traffic at this time was fish bait, and in 1931 it was reported that large numbers of lug worms were being gathered at Wells and sent to Yarmouth, Lowestoft and Southwold by passenger train; these unfortunate creatures were packed in wooden boxes and conveyed in the guard's compartments of ordinary trains – up to 10,000 worms being despatched each week during the winter months.

Most intermediate stations were equipped with cattle docks, end-loading bays, coal wharves and goods sheds, while some stations had fixed yard cranes capable of lifting containers, timber, drain pipes and other types of freight from rail to road vehicles. In addition, several stations had private industrial sidings for dealing with the area's important agricultural products, and one of these "lineside industries" was at Ryburgh, where the maltings were among the biggest in Norfolk. There were also rail-connected granaries, malt houses or other installations at Wells, Fakenham, Dereham, Hardingham and Yaxham, together with a dairy at North Elmham. The following table (compiled with the aid of the 1938 Railway Clearing House *Handbook of Stations*) gives some indication of the freight facilities available between Wymondham and Wells-on-Sea.

Table 3
GOODS AND PASSENGER ACCOMMODATION ON THE WYMONDHAM–WELLS BRANCH

Station	*Facilities*	*Crane*	*Private Sidings*
Wymondham	G P F L H C	1 ton	various quarry sidings
Kimberley Park	G P	–	–
Hardingham	G P F L H C	1 ton	Baly & Sons' siding
Thuxton	G P	–	–
Yaxham	G P L H	1 ton 10 cwt	granary
Dereham	G P F L H C	6 ton	mills, granaries & gas works
North Elmham	G P F L H C	1 ton	United Dairies
County School	G P	–	–
Ryburgh	G P F L H C	1 ton	F. & G. Smith's Maltings
Fakenham	G P F L H C	3 tons	Parker's Granary
Walsingham	G P F L H C	1 ton 10 cwt	–
Wells-on-Sea	G P F L H C	1 ton 10 cwt	granaries, quay sidings & a lime works

Key G = goods; P = passengers & parcels; F = loading docks for cars, furniture, portable machines, etc.; L = livestock; H = horses; C = carriages & motor cars by passenger train.

NORWICH, WYMONDHAM, DEREHAM, KING'S LYNN, and WELLS-ON-SEA.

Miles	Down.	Week Days. mrn	mrn	mrn	mrn	mrn Z		aft	aft T	aft	aft S	aft S	aft	aft	aft	aft S			Sundays. aft				
	Norwich (Thorpe) ....dep.	6 20	7 56	8 17	1038	1124	..	1 4	..	3 10	..	3 55	5 30	6 38	7 40	9 15	..	..	7 9	..	..	..	..
1	Trowse	6 24	8 0	8 21	1042	..	..	1 8	..	3 14	..	..	5 34	6 42	7 44	..	..	..	..	..	..	..	..
6¼	Hethersett	6 34	8 10	Dd	1053	..	..	1 19	..	3 25	..	..	5 45	6 53	7 55	9 26	..	..	7 20	..	..	..	..
10¼	Wymondham 874 ..arr.	6 42	8 18	8 39	11 1	1140	..	1 27	..	3 34	..	4 13	5 53	7 1	8 2	9 33	..	..	7 27	..	..	..	..
—	860London A 874..dep.	..	..	5 0	5 56	8‡15	..	10 3	‡	1225	..	1225	2 40	3 40	5 16	5 49	..	..	3 33	..	..	..	..
—	Wymondham ....dep	6 44	8 20	8 41	11 3	1141	..	1 29	..	3 38	..	4 15	5 54	7 3	8 9	9 34	..	..	7 29	..	..	..	..
14	Kimberley Park B	6 51	8 27	..	1110	..	..	1 36	..	3 46	..	4 22	6 1	7 10	8 16	9 41	..	..	7 36	..	..	..	..
15¾	Hardingham	6 56	8 32	8 51	1115	..	..	1 41	..	3 52	..	4 27	6 6	7 15	8 21	9 46	..	..	7 41	..	..	..	..
17¼	Thuxton	7 0	8 36	..	1119	..	..	1 45	..	3 57	..	4 31	6 10	7 19	8 25	9 50	..	..	7 45	..	..	..	..
19¾	Yaxham	7 6	8 42	..	1125	..	..	1 51	..	4 4	..	4 37	6 16	7 25	8 31	9 56	..	..	7 51	..	..	..	..
21¼	Dereham ....arr.	7 11	8 47	9 1	1130	1158	..	1 56	..	4 9	..	4 42	6 21	7 30	8 36	10 1	..	..	7 56	..	..	..	..
—	Dereham ....dep	7 25	..	9 6	1133	12 4	..	2 1	..	4 16	..	4 47	One class only.	7 33	Stop	..	..	..	..	..	..	..	..
25¾	Wendling	7 32	..	9 14	1140	..	..	2 8	..	4 24	..	4 54		7 40		..	..	..	..	..	..	..	..
28¼	Fransham	7 37	..	9 20	1145	..	..	2 13	..	4 31	..	5 0		7 45	..	..	..	..	..	..	..	..	..
29¾	Dunham	7 41	..	9 25	1149	..	..	2 17	..	4 37	..	5 4		7 49	..	..	..	..	..	..	..	..	..
33¾	Swaffham 879	7 53	..	9 37	1158	1222	..	2 26	One class only.	4 47	..	5 12		7 58	..	..	..	..	..	..	..	..	..
39¼	Narborough & Pentney..	8 2	..	9 46	12 6	1230	..	2 34		4 57	..	5 21		8 6	..	..	..	..	..	..	..	..	..
43	East Winch [1081, 1082	8 9	..	9 53	1213	1236	..	2 41		5 6	..	5 27		8 13	..	..	..	..	..	..	..	..	..
45	Middleton Towers [882,	8 13	..	9 58	1217	..	..	2 45		5 11	..	5 32	..	8 17	..	..	..	..	..	..	..	..	..
48¼	King's Lynn 881, arr.	8 21	..	10 4	1224	1245	..	2 51		5 20	..	5 38	..	8 24	..	..	..	..	..	..	..	..	..
89¾	881Cambridge......arr.	9 52	H	1144	..	..	..	4 37		6 57	..	6 57	..	12Y51	aft	..	..	..	..	..	..	..	..
145½	881London (Liv. St.) "	1119	H	2 5	..	..	..	6 10		8 20	..	8 20	..	2Y40	M	..	..	..	..	..	..	..	..
—	Dereham ....dep.	7 17	..	9 9	1134	..	..	2 0	3 2	4E21	4 35	4 46	..	7 34	8 40	10 5	..	..	8 0	..	..	..	..
26½	North Elmham	7 29	..	9 17	1142	..	..	2 8	3 10	4E29	4 43	4 54	..	7 42	8 48	1013	..	..	8X13	..	..	..	..
27¾	County School	7 34	..	9 22	1147	..	..	2 14	3 15	4E34	4 47	4 59	..	7 47	8 53	1020	..	..	8 18	..	..	..	..
31½	Ryburgh	7 42	..	9 29	1154	..	..	2 21	3 22	4E41	..	5 6	..	7 54	9 0	1027	..	..	8 25	..	..	..	..
33¾	Fakenham C 1082	7A58	..	9 37	12 1	..	..	2 28	3 27	4E47	..	5 13	..	8 0	9 7	1033	..	..	8 31	..	..	..	..
38¾	Walsingham	8 9	..	9 48	1212	..	..	2 39	..	4E58	..	5 25	..	8 11	9 18	1044	..	..	8 45	..	..	..	..
40¾	Wighton Halt*	8 14	..	9 53	1217	..	..	2 44	..	5E3	..	5 30	..	8 16	..	1049	..	..	8 50	..	..	..	..
46¼	Wells-on-Sea 878 ....arr.	8 21	..	10 0	1224	..	..	2 51	..	5E10	..	5 37	..	8 23	9 28	1056	..	..	8 57	..	..	..	..

Miles	Up.	Week Days. mrn	mrn	mrn	mrn	mrn S	mrn S		aft	aft	aft T	aft Z	aft	aft E	aft S	aft		aft	Sundays. aft				
	Wells-on-Sea ....dep.	5m52	..	7 33	9 7	..	1137		B1248	3 16	..	..	..	5 54	6 8	..	..	..	4 50	..	..	..	..
2¼	Wighton Halt*	..	..	7 39	9 13	..	1143		B1254	3 22	..	..	..	6 0	6 14	..	..	..	4 56	..	..	..	..
4¼	Walsingham	6m 2	..	7 45	9 19	..	1149	..	1B0	3 28	..	..	..	6 7	6 21	..	..	..	5 3	..	..	..	..
9½	Fakenham C 1082	6m12	..	7 55	9 37	..	12 2	..	1B10	3 38	4 18	..	..	6 20	6 33	..	..	..	5 14	..	..	..	..
12	Ryburgh	6m17	..	8 0	9 42	..	12 7	..	1B15	3 43	4 24	..	..	6 25	6 38	..	..	..	5 20	..	..	..	..
15½	County School 886	6m24	..	8 7	9 49	..	1214	..	1B22	3 50	4 34	..	6 3	6 32	6 45	7 50	..	..	5 27	..	..	..	..
17	North Elmham	6m29	..	8 12	9 57	..	1222	..	1 30	3 55	4 39	..	6 8	6 37	6 50	7 55	..	..	5 36	..	..	..	..
21¼	Dereham (above).....arr.	6m37	..	8 20	10 5	..	1230	..	1 38	4 3	4 47	..	6 16	6 45	6 58	8 3	..	..	5 44	..	..	..	..
—	881London (L.S.) dep.	..	..	..	..	5 56	..	..	8 30	1155	..	..	..	2 40	2 40		..	5 45	..	..	..	..	..
—	881Cambridge "	..	..	..	..	8P18	..	P	1020	1 22	..	1P27	..	4 5	4 15		..	7 15	..	..	..	..	..
—	King's Lynn.....dep.	..	..	7 20	9 4	1030	..	..	1245	3 14	One class only.	4 5	..	5 48	6 3	One class only	..	8 49	..	..	..	..	..
— 3¼	Middleton Towers	..	..	7 27	9 11	..	..	..	1251	3 20		..	..	5 54	6 9		..	8 56	..	..	..	..	..
— 5¼	East Winch	..	..	7 32	9 16	..	..	..	1256	3 25		..	..	5 59	6 14		..	9 1	..	..	..	..	..
— 8¼	Narborough & Pentney	..	..	7 38	9 22	1043	..	..	1 2	3 31		4 18	..	6 5	6 20		..	9 8	..	..	..	..	..
— 14½	Swaffham 879	..	..	7 52	9 37	1054	..	..	1 13	3 43		4 29	..	6 17	6 32		..	9 21	..	..	..	..	..
— 18½	Dunham	..	..	8 0	9 45	11 2	..	..	1 21	3 51		4 37	..	6 25	6 40		..	9 29	..	..	..	..	..
— 19¾	Fransham	..	..	8 4	9 49	..	..	..	1 25	3 55		..	..	6 29	6 44		..	9 33	..	..	..	..	..
— 22½	Wendling ....[886	..	..	8 10	9 55	1110	..	..	1 30	4 0		4 45	..	6 34	6 49		..	9 39	..	..	..	..	..
— 26¼	Dereham (above) arr.	..	..	8 17	10 2	1116	..	..	1 36	4 6		4 51	..	6 40	6 55		..	9 46	..	..	..	..	..
—	Dereham ....dep.	6 41	6 57	8 23	1011	1120	1232	..	1 41	4 13	4 48	4 55	6F36	6 49	7 2	8 25	..	9 51	5 47	..	..	..	..
23½	Yaxham	6 46	..	8 28	1016	1125	1237	..	1 46	4 18	..	..	..	6 54	7 7	8 30	..	9R56	5 52	..	..	..	..
26	Thuxton	6 52	..	8 34	1022	1131	1243	..	1 52	4 24	..	..	6F45	7 1	7 13	8 36	..	..	5 59	..	..	..	..
27½	Hardingham	6 56	7 7	8 38	1026	1135	1247	..	1 56	4 28	..	..	6F49	7 5	7 17	8 40	..	..	6 3	..	..	..	..
29¼	Kimberley Park B [874	7 1	..	8 43	1031	1140	1252	..	2 1	4 33	..	..	6F54	7 11	7 23	8 45	..	..	6 10	..	..	..	..
33	Wymondham 862 ..arr.	7 7	7 16	8 49	1041	1146	1258	..	2 7	4 39	5 6	5 11	7F2	7 17	7 29	8 51	..	1010	6 17	..	..	..	..
147	862London (L.St) 874arr	10n23	1023	1235	2V14	..	4‡57	..	5 19	8 20	8 20	8 20	11F38	11N24	11N24	..	..	2 40	9 41	..	..	..	..
—	Wymondham ....dep.	7 9	8F9	8 52	1044	1147	1259	..	2 10	4 42	5 7	5 12	..	7 20	7 31	8 52	..	1012	6 19	..	..	..	..
37	Hethersett	7 20	8F18	9 1	1053	..	1 8	..	2 19	4 51	..	..	..	7 29	7 40	9 1	..	..	6 28	..	..	..	..
42¼	Trowse ....[884	7 29	8F26	9 9	11 1	..	1 16	..	2 27	4 59	..	..	..	7 37	7 48	9 9	..	1025	..	..	..	..	..
43¾	Norwich (Thorpe) 882 arr	7 33	8F30	9 13	11 5	12 3	1 20	..	2 31	5 3	5 25	5 28	..	7 41	7 52	9 13	..	1029	6 38	..	..	..	..

A Liverpool Street.
A Arrives at 7 47 mrn.
B Station for Hingham (3 miles).
B .. mins. later on Sats.
C Over ¾ mile to Mid. & G. N. Joint Station.
Dd Stops at 8 32 mrn. when required to take up for beyond Dereham.
E or E Except Saturdays.
F One class only.
H Arr. Cambridge 11 54 mrn. and London (L. St.) 2 9 aft. on Sats.

M or m Mondays only.
N King's Cross Station.
n Arr 10 18 mrn Mons.
P Via March.
R Stops when required to set down.
S Saturdays only.
T Thurs. only.
T Arrives at 9 28 mrn.
V 5 mins. later on Sats. Passengers can arrive 2 10 aft., via Norwich.
X Arr. 8 7 aft.
Y Via March except on Sats.
Z Tues. only.

* Passengers to or from Wighton (Halt) must travel in the compartment next to the guards van.
‡ Via Norwich.

Other Trains

Norwich and Wymondham.......862
Dereham and County School.....886
Norwich and County School.....886

Bradshaw Timetable for March 1938.

Pre-War Developments

Apart from the progressive introduction of bogie passenger stock, the LNER made one or two other changes and improvements during the 1930s. Wells station, for example, was substantially rebuilt, with a new connection between the Wells & Fakenham and West Norfolk portions of the terminus. Hitherto, the only connection between what were in effect two separate stations had been a single crossover; the new connection supplemented this by diverging southwards from the West Norfolk line and rejoining the Fakenham line near the signal box. The passenger station was rebuilt at about the same time, with new platforms, improved lighting and an extended overall roof (*see Chapter 5* for details). Another innovation was the opening of Wighton Halt to serve the village of Wighton (roughly midway between Wells and Walsingham); this simple, passenger-only stopping place appeared in the timetables in 1923. One small alteration carried out in the 1930s was a change of name from "Wells" to "Wells-on-Sea" – presumably in an attempt to prevent confusion with the Great Western station at Wells in Somerset.

The main development at this time was not however initiated by the LNER, but by certain "High Church" elements within the Church of England. Until the Protestant Reformation, Walsingham had rivalled Canterbury as a centre of Christian pilgrimage, but in the 1530s the monasteries were abolished, and the Shrine of "Our Lady of Walsingham" was dismantled – its "graven images of silver and gold" being symbolically burned at Smithfield. Thereafter the Church of England remained visibly Protestant in its forms of service, and only in the 19th Century did incense, stained glass, plaster saints, genuflection and other supposedly "Catholic" practices became acceptable. At its most extreme, "High Church" Anglicism developed into a form of Anglo-Catholicism which was, in most respects, identical to traditional Catholicism. Inevitably, Anglo-Catholics were eager to repair what they saw as the damage of the Reformation, and with this thought in mind an Anglican shrine was opened at Walsingham in 1931. Walsingham pilgrimages became so popular that in 1938 the original shrine was enlarged to accommodate the growing number of visitors.

Meanwhile, the Roman Catholics had established a shrine of their own in the historic "Slipper Chapel" at Houghton St Giles, and in 1934 no less than 12,000 people travelled to Walsingham for a service at the restored shrine. For the first time in its history, the Wells branch became an important excursion destination, and in the next few years special trains were run to Walsingham from London and other large cities (further details of Walsingham and "Slipper Chapel Halt" will be found in the next chapter).

Unfortunately, this renewed interest in Walsingham did not contribute towards a sudden growth in holiday traffic to Wells, and the LNER never treated the little town as a seaside resort. In 1931 for instance, the company's annual publicity material featured a map of Eastern England together with the slogan, "LNER for the DRIER SIDE"; significantly, Wells-on-Sea was omitted from this map though the neighbouring resorts of Hunstanton, Sheringham and Cromer were clearly marked. Only in terms of excursion traffic could Wells claim to be a "holiday" resort, and at the height of Summer there was a considerable flow of *day* trippers from Dereham and Norwich.

Like most branch lines, the Wells branch served the surrounding area in perfect safety for over a Century, but on 27th May, 1931 Fakenham was the scene of an accident which could easily have been disastrous. The platform layout at that station included a dead end bay on the down side which could be used by services starting or terminating journeys between Fakenham and Norwich. On the day in question the bay was occupied by an 'E4' 2–4–0 and a train consisting of bogie vehicles and 6-wheel coaches. The turnouts – and presumably all signals – were set for the bay but another 'E4', heading a down passenger train (which was approaching Fakenham from the south) ran past the down signal and crashed into the stationary train. The locomotives involved in the collision were Nos. 7457 and 7486, and although not badly damaged both were subsequently scrapped (one assumes that their age made repairs unworthwhile). Fortunately, the down working had been slowing prior to stopping in Fakenham station, but this slow speed could not prevent the death of one person and injuries to a further nineteen travellers.

World War Two

On Sunday 3rd September, 1939 the people of Wells, Fakenham and the surrounding area heard Prime Minister Neville Chamberlain's radio announcement that Britain had declared war on Germany. Many listeners expected the blue Norfolk skies to fill with Luftwaffe bombers within the first few days, but in the event the initial months of the conflict were so quiet that people talked of a "Phoney War". For railway travellers, a reduction in services, a nightly blackout and the sight of soldiers hurrying to join their units was the only sign that there was a "war on".

The sudden and unexpected collapse of France in June 1940 dispelled any illusions about the gravity of the situation, and with a broad swathe of land from Sussex to the Wash declared an emergency area, the people of north Norfolk found themselves in the "front line" of a major conflict. Road signs and station nameboards were taken down, beaches were mined, and obstructions were placed in fields and open spaces to impede airborne landings. All able-bodied males were encouraged to join the Local Defence Volunteers (renamed the Home Guard in July 1940) and – at a time when invasion was thought to be imminent – these part-time soldiers could be seen guarding beaches, railway bridges and other installations in the area.

Less visibly, a secretive force of elite Home Guard "Special Units" was preparing to wage guerrilla warfare on the event of a successful landing. Consisting mainly of local farmers, poachers, gamekeepers and other specialists, the Special Units had made elaborate plans, and, although these preparations are still secret, there can be little doubt that the Wells branch would itself have become a target for sabotage as soon as it fell into enemy hands. (It is rumoured that the large embankment at East Barsham would have been blown up to sever the line at a particularly inconvenient place.)

It was at this critical phase of the war that armoured trains were brought into play in order to counteract Britain's acute shortage of conventional guns and armoured vehicles, and, like other coastal lines, the Wells-next-the-Sea branch was patrolled regularly by one of these hastily-assembled units. The train consisted of former GER 'F4' class 2–4–2T No. 7189 flanked by two low sided general purpose wagons and two LMS steel 20 ton coal wagons; locomotive and coal wagons were protected by ¼ inch steel plate, and the entire train was camouflaged. Offensive armament consisted of rifles, machine guns and naval 6 pounders – the latter being mounted in the armoured wagons in such a way that a 240 degree arc of fire was possible ahead and astern of the train. When on patrol the train carried a crew of twenty-six, including gunners, wireless operators and locomen.

There were in all a grand total of twenty such trains, each one being given a distinguishing letter of the alphabet. Train "G" was allocated to the North Norfolk area and in July 1940 it started to patrol the area between Kings Lynn and Great Yarmouth, making regular trips along the Wells branch and the West Norfolk line. The train was stationed, for much of the war, at Heacham, from where it made regular patrols to both Hunstanton and Wells-next-the-Sea, and it was while on one of these patrols that Train "G" collided with a rake of stationary coaches at Wells with such force that the locomotive broke its buffer beam. It is interesting to recall that, for at least part of its wartime career, Train "G" was manned exclusively by Polish Army officers, who (like their fellow countrymen in the RAF) welcomed any chance to participate in the allied war effort after the tragic defeat of their own country in 1940.

Historians now agree that Hitler never seriously intended to invade Britain, but on the other hand he hoped that the *threat* of invasion, coupled with heavy air attacks, would force Britain into an armistice so that the Germans could invade Russia. As we now know, the attack on Russia went ahead in June 1941, leaving Britain undefeated in the West, and able to bomb Hitler's Europe from the air. As far as the Wells branch was concerned, this second phase of the war was dominated by a vast build-up of British air power in East Anglia, and like other local lines it carried a heavy traffic in RAF (and later USAAF) personnel to and from local aerodromes such as RAF Langham and RAF North Creake. Many of these airfields were bomber stations; North Creake, for example, was a Bomber Command support station operating Stirling heavy bombers. RAF Little Snoring (3 miles north east of Fakenham) was a similar establishment which (by 1944) was operating the famous Mosquito fighter bombers. Langham, in contrast, was a Coastal Command station equipped with Beaufighters. Other local aerodromes included RAF Scuthorpe, RAF Foulsham, RAF Swanton Morley, RAF Wendling and RAF Shipdham – all of which were situated within a mile or two of the Wymondham to Wells line.

With so many legitimate military targets in the immediate vicinity, it was perhaps inevitable that the Luftwaffe would bomb the area, and on one of these enemy raids – on August Bank Holiday Monday 1941 – Ryburgh railway station was hit. The target, on this occasion, was probably Little Snoring airfield rather than the railway – though the latter must have made an ideal navigational feature for the enemy pilots. In fact the Germans managed to inflict considerable damage, not just to railway property but also to the adjoining maltings; the remains of the station were afterwards demolished. Norwich, too, was badly hit during several German air raids, which caused considerable damage to Norwich Thorpe station.

Quite apart from any physical damage, such air raids obviously caused delays and disruptions to ordinary train services – and all of this took place at a time when the railways were struggling to carry extra traffic. Branch trains were, at this time packed with service personnel from all over the British Isles, and the accents of Northern England, the Midlands, Scotland, Ireland and Wales could be heard in every train and on every station, interspersed with the distinctive yet familiar Norfolk drawl. Commonwealth accents could be heard too, for there were numerous Canadian, Australian and New Zealand airmen in the area; indeed, there was quite a concentration of Antipodean airmen around Wells, and by 1944 RAF Langham had one RAAF and one RNZAF Squadron!

In physical terms the war produced few changes, the extensive track layouts at most intermediate stations being adequate for the needs of most wartime traffic. Apart from the influx of military personnel, the line carried vast quantities of building material – most of which was used to build runways. Dereham became an important marshalling centre during the peak of airfield construction, and additional sidings were installed for this important wartime traffic; at one period Dereham was handling no less than 75 wagon loads of construction materials each day.

The end of the war in Europe was followed by the election of Mr Attlee's Labour government, and on 1st January, 1948 a nationwide fanfare of locomotive whistles heralded the demise of the "Big Four" main line companies and the birth of BRITISH RAILWAYS – the new, nationally-owned railway organisation; as in 1923, an era had come to an end.

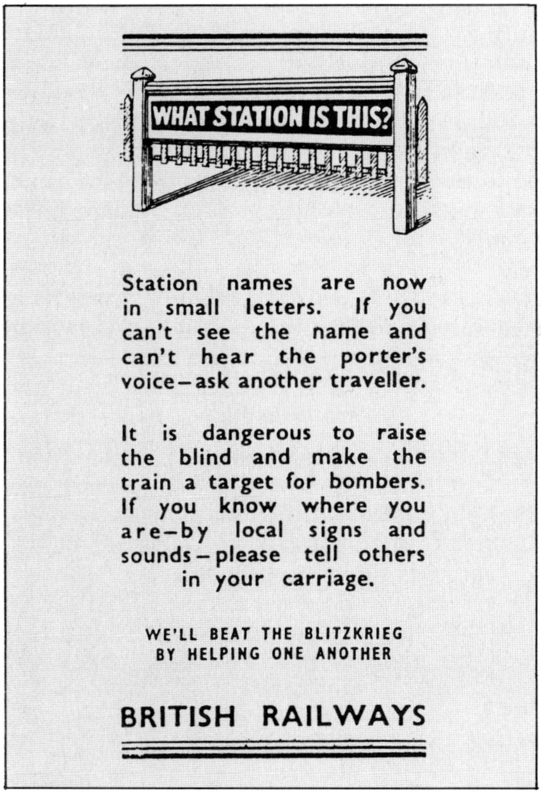

Chapter Five

The Route Described

Wells trains commenced their journeys at Norwich Thorpe, where the station, opened in 1844, had been the original western terminus of the Yarmouth & Norwich Railway; trains from Brandon and Newport shared the station from 15th December, 1845, by which date the Yarmouth & Norwich and Norwich & Brandon companies had combined to form the Norfolk Railway. The Eastern Union Railway opened a separate terminus at Norwich Victoria in 1849, but in 1862, when the Great Eastern Railway was formed, Norwich Thorpe became the city's main terminal station. The station was extensively rebuilt in 1886, as a result of which it acquired an impressive façade of somewhat "Central European" appearance. Behind its towering dome and ornate *porte-cochère,* however, it remained an essentially simple affair, with six dead-end platforms serving trains to London, Yarmouth, Lowestoft, Cromer, Kings Lynn and Wells.

Leaving Norwich Thorpe, trains soon came to Thorpe Junction, where Yarmouth workings diverged eastwards; beyond, the line continued to Trowse Lower Junction – at which point London services turned right to reach Trowse Upper Junction and the Liverpool Street main line. Heading south-west, Wells trains entered a deep cutting, over which the main line passed on an impressive arched viaduct. The route then turned onto a westerly heading and, running through Hethersett station without stopping, trains reached Wymondham, 10 miles 18 chains from Norwich and the junction for Wells and Forncett. (It is interesting to note that, although northbound trains between Norwich and Wells were designated "down" workings, they ran on the up main line as far as the junction at Wymondham, calling *en route* in the up platform.)

Wymondham

Serving a small but busy country town, Wymondham station had three platforms – the up side being an island with two faces. The main station buildings were on the down side, and there were smaller waiting rooms on the up platform; an attractive footbridge linked both platforms and the station approach road. Nearby, there were several sidings serving roadstone quarries. Other features here included the usual cattle dock, goods shed and loading docks, together with a small engine shed (sub to Norwich) and a 45 ft diameter turntable.

Kimberley Park

From Wymondham, trains diverged north-westwards onto the Dereham line, passing Wymondham South Junction signal box and

Although it occupied the approximate site of the original Norfolk Railway terminus, Norwich Thorpe was relatively modern, and dated from 1886 (the original terminus then became a goods yard). The station was bombed by the German Luftwaffe in World War Two, and evidence of the resulting damage can be seen in this *c.*1958 view. *Lens of Sutton*

A view of Norwich Thorpe in the 1950s, with a Metro Cammell dmu set just visible beneath the overall roof; apart from the new lamps, the station looks much as it did before the First World War! *Lens of Sutton*

An Edwardian view of the main station buildings at Wymondham, as railwaymen, travellers and cabmen pose in the sun for the plate camera. The attractive brick-and-flint buildings were similar to others on the former Norfolk Railway. *Lens of Sutton*

A general view of Wymondham station, looking west in British Railways days. *Lens of Sutton*

A general view of the west end of Wymondham station, showing the main running lines in the centre and the Dereham/Wells branch diverging to the right.
C.L. Mowat Collection

A general view of Wymondham station, looking east in British Railways days.
Lens of Sutton

Kimberley station looking south towards Wymondham in September 1969. The two storey building, with its steeply pitched roof, was the original Norfolk Railway station, while the more modern-looking waiting room and canopy in the foreground was a GER addition, bearing the company's initials in its ornate iron work. The train arriving is the 12.35 Dereham to Norwich local service. *G.R. Mortimer*

The desolation of Kimberley station after rationalisation. *Lens of Sutton*

An Edwardian view of Hardingham station; unfortunately this photograph does not show the wagon turntable, which is hidden from view by the platform. *Lens of Sutton*

A rear view of the attractive Jacobean-style station buildings at Hardingham. *Lens of Sutton*

Thuxton station looking south towards Norwich in September 1969. Thuxton was similar to other stations between Wymondham and Dereham, and had the same "Tudor Gothic" type buildings, together with later GER additions giving increased passenger accommodation. *G.R. Mortimer*

Yaxham looking north towards Wells-next-the-Sea, and showing the Norfolk Railway buildings (*left*) and GE waiting rooms (*right*). Unusually, the signal cabin adjoined the up side buildings. *G.R. Mortimer*

Detail of Yaxham station, showing a post box, and "LNER" fire bucket in October 1969. *G.R. Mortimer*

Yaxham signal cabin was a typical GE gabled structure – though it was slightly taller than usual in order to provide a clear view over the adjoining waiting room. Photographed in October 1969 during the last week of passenger service. *G.R. Mortimer*

The main station buildings at Dereham, seen from Station Road. Note the fine chimneys in this 1910 view. *Lens of Sutton*

The northern extremity of Dereham's down platform, with maltings and other lineside industries visible in the distance. *Lens of Sutton*

immediately entering a cutting. Nearing the village of Crownthorpe, the double track branch turned westwards, and running through a succession of cuttings and embankments, trains soon arrived at Kimberley Park, the first intermediate station.

Situated some 13 miles 77 chains from Norwich, this small station served the village of Kimberley – which was about half a mile to the north; two platforms were provided, with the main station buildings on the up side and a small, single siding goods yard on the down side of the line. Until 1923 the station was called simply "Kimberley", but after the Grouping its name was changed to Kimberley Park to avoid confusion with a former GNR station serving Kimberley in Nottinghamshire. The station master here in 1912 was Mr W. Tallent, who had previously served at County School and later transferred to Hardingham.

Architecturally, Kimberley Park was (like the rest of the stations between Wymondham and Dereham) of great interest and charm – indeed, its ornate, Tudor style buildings would not have been out of place at a much larger station. Built in at least two distinct stages, these buildings incorporated a variety of materials and construction methods, including brick, brick-and-flint, stucco, timber, and iron. The main block contained a two storey station master's dwelling, which was situated at right angles to the platform; smaller wings extended from each side, while a glass-fronted waiting room provided additional accommodation for the travelling public.

Hardingham

Departing from Kimberley Park, trains crossed the B1108 road on the level, and reaching a short section of embankment, passed over an occupation bridge. Climbing steadily, the route turned imperceptibly to the north west before entering a series of cuttings which extended almost as far as Hardingham (15 miles 60 chains), the next stopping place. Similar in many ways to Kimberley, Hardingham was another two-platform station, with extensive, Jacobean-style buildings on its down side. There were several sidings in the goods yard, and other facilities included a rail-connected granary, a cattle dock, and a standard GER gabled signal cabin; an archaic wagon turntable remained *in situ* in the goods yard until recent years.

Thuxton

Leaving Hardingham, Wells trains headed north-westwards, with the River Yare to the right and the B1135 running parallel to the left. Thuxton, the next stop (17 miles 10 chains), was an attractive country station with a level crossing to the south of its two platforms and a small goods yard on the down side. The station buildings were on the down platform, and like their counterparts at Kimberley and Hardingham, these structures exhibited an interesting mixture of architectural styles; the main block, with its two storey station master's house and quaint "Tudor" style details, was presumably of Norfolk Railway origin, but the detached, brick-and-timber waiting room was of obvious Great Eastern appearance and displayed the letters "GER" in its cast iron spandrels.

Yaxham

Continuing north-westwards the double track railway passed within a quarter of a mile of the village of Garveston, beyond which the route ran first on embankments and then through cuttings before eventually reaching Yaxham, 19 miles 59 chains from Norwich. Up and down platforms were provided here, the main station building being on the down side. The goods yard contained a large, gabled goods shed, and there was a level crossing to the north of the platforms. Further sidings diverged from the down side of the line in order to serve an adjacent granary, and it was possible – via a connection between the up main line and the granary headshunt – for southbound goods trains to reverse across the down main line to pick-up loaded vehicles from this private siding.

Yaxham's relatively complex track layout was controlled by a Great Eastern style signal box which was (unusually) attached to a range of brick-and-timber waiting rooms. The box itself was of typical GER appearance, and was built to that company's usual pre-fabricated design. Yaxham box was slightly taller than most of the other boxes between Wymondham and Wells, but it was in most respects a typical specimen, measuring a standard 24 ft x 12 ft at ground level. The adjacent level crossing was also of typical Great Eastern design, with a single set of gates which – being of great size and weight – needed diagonal bracing and massive, white-painted gate posts. (Although primarily a structural feature, these prominent white posts also gave engine drivers a useful visual identification when approaching each crossing.)

Dereham

From Yaxham, the route fell slightly into the Tud Valley and crossed the River Tud – little more than a stream at this point – on a small bridge before burrowing into the opposite hillside by means of another cutting. Nearing Dereham, trains passed the quaintly-named hamlet of Dumpling Green, where, in 1803, the writer George Borrow had been born; cuttings prevented a clear view, but a few houses could be glimpsed in the distance as the train crossed the B1135 road on the level. Nearing Dereham, the route forked; to the left a south-to-west curve provided a direct route to Kings Lynn for freight and excursion trains, but passenger workings continued straight on past the west to north curve which converged from the left, and immediately entered the main down platform at Dereham, 21 miles 51 chains from Norwich.

Although East Dereham was merely a small country town, its station was a place of some importance, shared by trains to Wroxham, Kings Lynn and Wells-next-the-Sea. Long up and down platforms were provided, together with an additional bay on the down side. The extensive, Jacobean-style station buildings were on the down platform – which was considerably longer than its counterpart on the up side. Both platforms were partially covered by canopies, and the station boasted a privately-run refreshment room. Goods facilities were equally lavish, and included a large goods shed on the up side, several sidings, a cattle dock, and a 6-ton crane. Additionally, private sidings served Dereham gas works, Whitbread's Maltings, Fison & Sons, and various other agricultural premises.

Many trains were divided at Dereham, the usual practice being for the front portion to continue to Wells, while the rearmost vehicles were taken to Kings Lynn behind another locomotive. These operations gave Dereham an atmosphere of bustle and activity which was perhaps unusual at such a rural station. Underlining its importance as a local traffic centre, Dereham had a small engine shed, which usually accommodated 'E4' 2–4–0s, 'J15' 0–6–0s or other former GER locomotives.

North Elmham

Continuing northwards, Wells trains ran through the eastern environs of Dereham, passing over three closely-spaced level crossings in quick succession. The double track ended at Dereham North Box, and drivers had to be in possession of a single line tablet before proceeding. Climbing slightly, the railway entered a cutting which was spanned by five overbridges – one of which carried a minor road leading from Dereham to the outlying hamlet of Northall Green. Surmounting a miniature summit, the route then descended on gradients as steep as 1 in 135, and with a minor road running parallel to the left trains entered the Wensum Valley. About 4 miles from Dereham the minor road turned to the right, crossing the railway on the level and then heading towards the nearby village of Worthing. North Elmham station was slightly less than a mile further on.

A small station, situated 16 miles 14 chains from Norwich, North Elmham had a single platform on the down side, with a level crossing to the south. A United Dairies milk depot was sited behind the

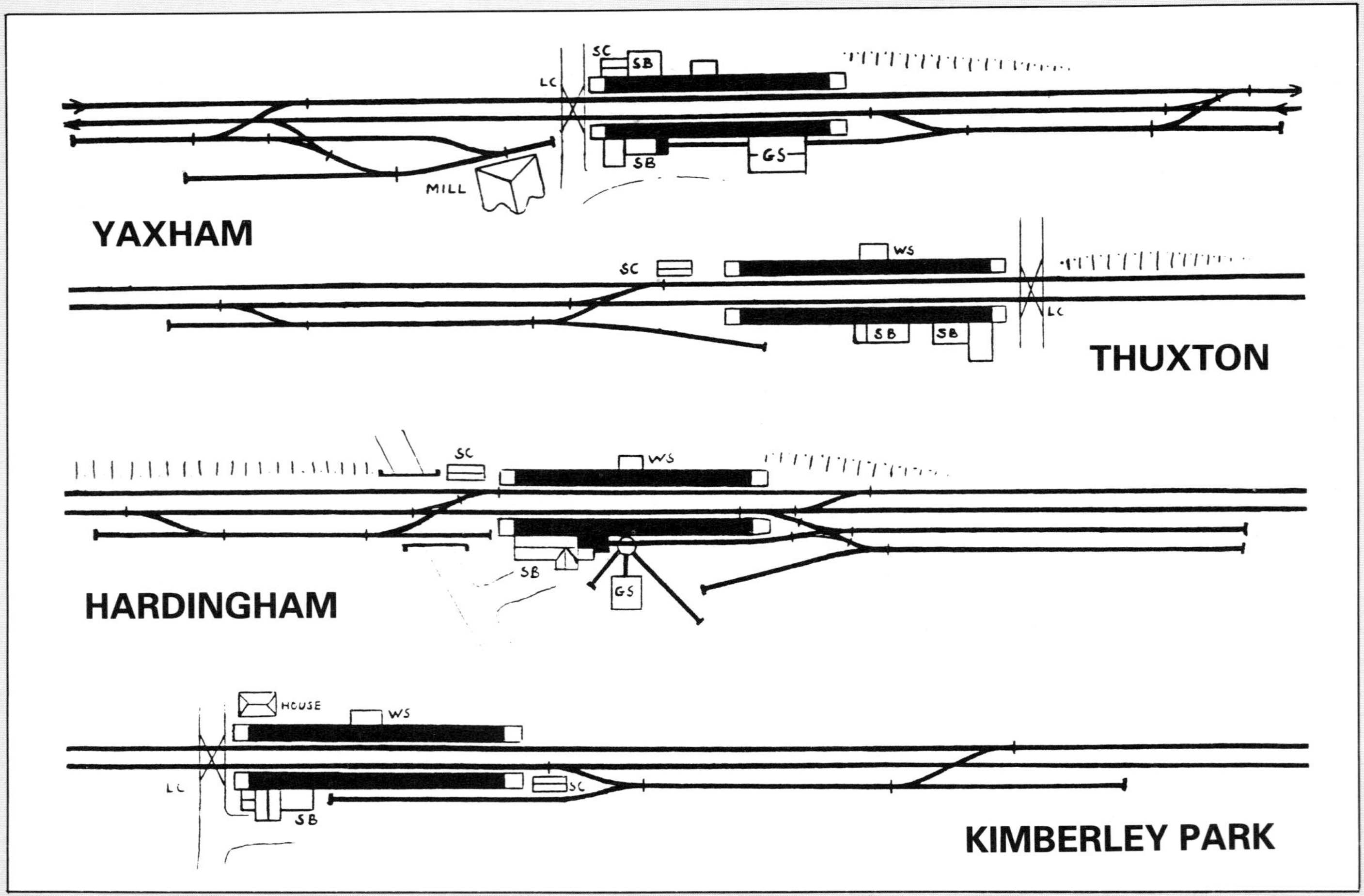

SC
SB
LC
SB
GS
MILL
YAXHAM
WS
SC
SB
SB
LC
THUXTON
SC
WS
SB
GS
HARDINGHAM
HOUSE
WS
LC
SC
SB
KIMBERLEY PARK

platform, and this was served by a single siding which formed a trailing connection with the "main line". Empty milk tanks could be backed into the siding by northbound trains, but this arrangement was inconvenient when loaded vehicles were picked up by southbound trains, and full milk tanks were collected from a separate siding on the up side of the line; a shunting horse was used to transfer these vehicles from one side of the line to the other. Passenger trains did not cross here, but the passing loop could if necessary be used by freight workings; the neat, brick-built station building dated from the LNER period.

Originally called "Elmham", the station served both North Elmham and nearby Worthing villages – though the passenger platform, being on the down side, was more convenient for North Elmham residents. (In situations where stations served two or more villages, Victorian railway companies invariably named their stations after the senior, though not necessarily the largest, village; thus North Elmham – the seat of an important Saxon Bishopric – inevitably took precedence over humble Worthing.)

Following the River Wensum, the line continued northwards, passing within half a mile of North Elmham's famous Saxon ruins (later incorporated into a 14th Century Bishop's Palace). County School, the next station, was only 1 mile 43 chains further on. The single line sections beyond North Elmham were all operated by the train staff and ticket system – which allowed successive trains to enter a single line provided that their respective drivers possessed written authorisation in lieu of a train staff; the staff itself would be carried by the last train in an up or down series. This method of single line control (which was merely a variant of the divisible staff or multiple staff systems) was particularly useful between County School and North Elmham, as this short section of line was used by Wroxham –Dereham services as well as Norwich–Wells workings.

County School

County School was an isolated, rural station, with up and down platforms and an additional bay for Wroxham services – some of which started or terminated their journeys here. Curiously, the distance from Norwich to County School via Wroxham (32 miles 31 chains) compared favourably with that via the Dereham line (27 miles 57 chains) though the latter was obviously the favoured route. The Norfolk County School was just a few hundred yards to the east of its station, and linked to it by a leafy carriage drive. In the Edwardian period, the school became "The Watts Naval Training School" – a branch of Dr Barnardo's Homes; apart from the school,

County School station served only scattered farms and cottages – the nearest village was North Elmham, around a mile to the south.

Amusingly, the station master during World War I had rejoiced in the vaguely-Biblical name of Gabriel Paynter, while (in continuation of the religious theme) one of his subordinates was called Mr Herod! Until 1912 the station master had been Walter Tallent – who enjoyed a long association with the Wells branch and served at several of its stations.

Accelerating past an impressive array of characteristically tall Great Eastern semaphores, trains headed north on what appeared to be a conventional double track section, but was in reality two single lines – the left hand track being the "main line" while the right hand line was the Wroxham branch. The two lines ran side by side for the next mile until the Wroxham route veered eastwards near the village of Broom Green. Occasionally a Dereham to Wroxham train would be shunted into the bay at County School in order to provide connections for those travelling north to Wells and, having made their connection, the two trains sometimes departed more or less simultaneously, resulting in what appeared to be a neck-and-neck "race" along the parallel lines. On these occasions schoolboy travellers would urge on their respective trains – knowing however that the Wells-bound "Claud" would always "win" when the Wroxham-bound 'E4' slowed for the sharp curve at Broom Green!

Ryburgh

As their trains left Broom Green travellers could, if they looked carefully to the right, discern what looked like an abandoned south to east curve; as far as can be ascertained this never carried any track – except possibly temporary contractor's lines used during construction of the Wroxham branch in the 1880s.

Climbing gradually, the railway headed north westwards beside the sparkling River Wensum, running first in a cutting and then on a low embankment. With attractively-wooded hillsides visible to the right, trains rumbled beneath a road overbridge and then entered a further cutting. Nearing Ryburgh, the line emerged onto another embankment which was pierced, at one point, by a small road under-bridge. Although the surrounding countryside was unspectacular, the rolling hills and ample woodlands ensured that it was never dull, and discerning travellers were treated to a continually changing panorama of rural English scenery at its best.

Ryburgh, 31 miles 21 chains, served the villages of Great Ryburgh (near the station) and Little Ryburgh (visible on higher ground to the north of the railway). Like North Elmham, it had a single platform on the down side and a level crossing to the south; large, rail-connected maltings on the down side provided a useful source of originating

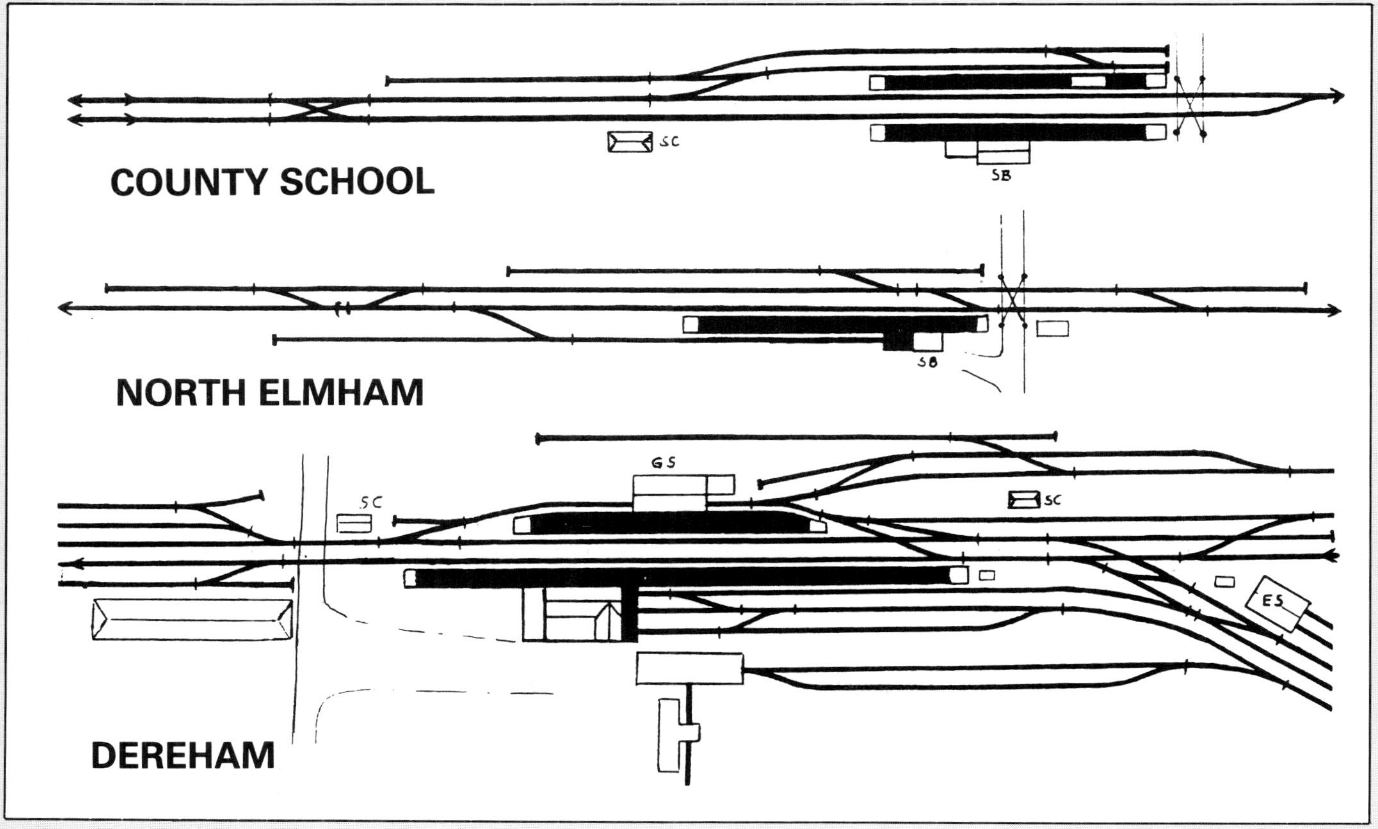

SC
SB
COUNTY SCHOOL
SB
NORTH ELMHAM
GS
SC
SC
ES
DEREHAM

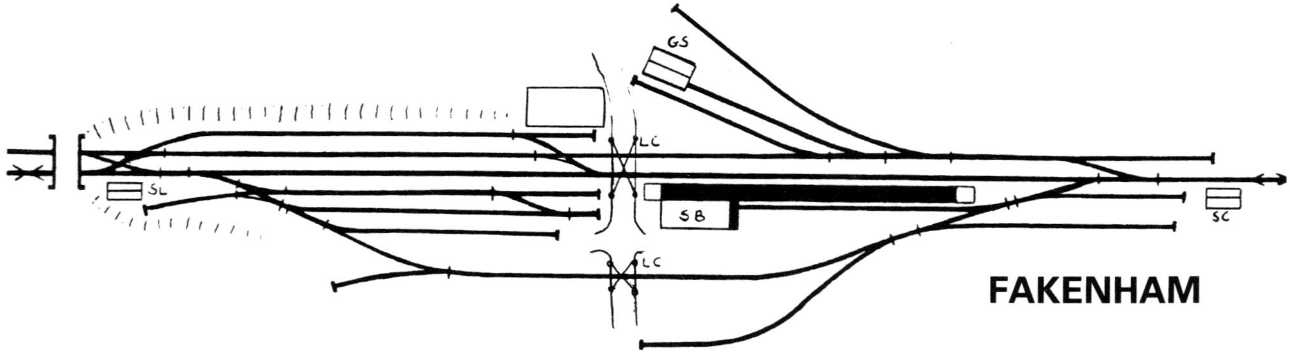

FAKENHAM

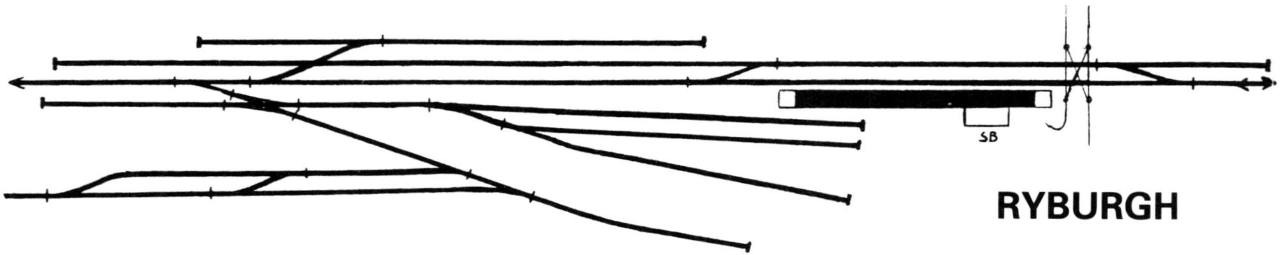

RYBURGH

traffic at this otherwise remote place. The surviving station buildings consisted of little more than a former porter's room, but in an attempt to hide the scars of World War II local railway staff had planted an attractive flower garden on the site of the bombed-out booking office and waiting room.

Fakenham

Beyond Ryburgh the line – still rising gently – curved onto a more westerly heading as it followed the south bank of the River Wensum. A glance to the right revealed the Midland & Great Northern line running parallel on the opposite bank of the river, and for the next mile the two lines ran side by side. Eventually, the GER route curved north-westwards and crossed first the river and then the M&GN before trains reached the GER station at Fakenham.

The principal intermediate station between Dereham and Wells, Fakenham was 33 miles 62 chains from Norwich and 23 miles 44 chains from Wymondham. Its track layout was relatively complex, although (perhaps surprisingly) there was only one long platform and a short bay on the down side; the main crossing loop was situated to the north of the platform and separated from it by an intervening level crossing.

Until 1928 the station had been controlled from two standard GER signal boxes, designated "Fakenham North" and "Fakenham South", but in later years the south box was abolished and thereafter all signals were controlled from the former north box. In operational terms Fakenham was especially important in so far as it was roughly half way between Dereham and Wells, and possessed the only passenger crossing loop between County School and the end of the line at Wells-next-the-Sea.

The station buildings here were a two storey, hip-roofed design, incorporating a station master's dwelling; the projecting platform canopy, with its large spandrels, was a later Great Eastern addition. Other facilities included the usual cattle pens, loading docks, a goods shed, and a 3 ton yard crane. The station was, throughout most of its life, known as "Fakenham", but after nationalisation BR renamed it "Fakenham *East*" to distinguish it from the Midland & Great Northern establishment at the other end of the town. Fakenham town centre was about half a mile to the west, and the tall tower of its Parish Church was a conspicuous local landmark.

Walsingham

Leaving Fakenham, northbound trains entered a substantial cutting and, passing beneath four road overbridges in rapid succes-

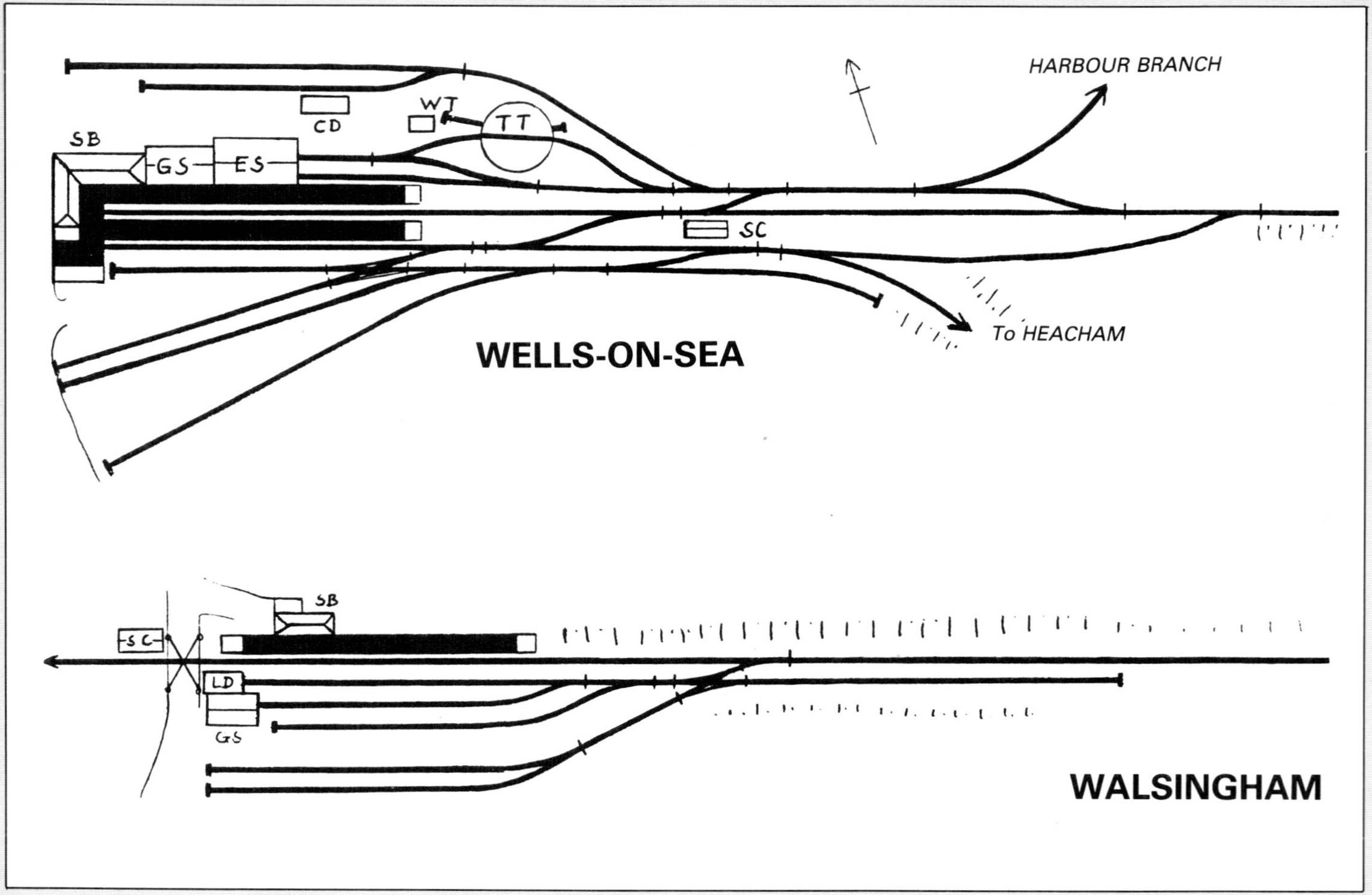

HARBOUR BRANCH
SB
GS
ES
CD
WT
TT
SC
To HEACHAM
WELLS-ON-SEA
SB
SC
LD
GS
WALSINGHAM

sion, commenced their 1 in 81 climb out of the Wensum Valley. With the staccato beat of the labouring engine leaving no doubt that the general direction was now upwards, the branch continued towards its summit. About 1½ miles beyond Fakenham, trains passed a rail-connected granary on the up side; access to the single siding was controlled by an Annett's Key carried on the Fakenham–Walsingham train staff. Continuing northwards the branch crossed first a minor road and then the B1105 on the level; it is interesting to record that the B1105 level crossing was protected by an ancient "crossbar" signal which indicated danger when the gates were closed across the railway. (This presumably dated from the Wells & Fakenham era.)

Reaching its modest summit elevation of approximately 175 ft the line then curved gradually north east towards the Stiffkey (pronounced "Stewkey") Valley. As their train crossed the valley travellers could, by glancing to the right, see the picturesque village of East Barsham with its archetypal Tudor manor house where, in 1511, King Henry VIII had lodged prior to walking (it is said) barefoot to the shrine of Our Lady of Walsingham.

As we have seen, the railway originally crossed the Stiffkey on a timber viaduct but this had been replaced by an embankment in the early 20th Century. It is interesting to recall a local legend which suggests that the old viaduct was actually *buried* rather than replaced; this would have been a sensible course of action, and the operation could have been carried out without serious disruption to traffic. The replacement embankment was pierced by a single arch bridge with a cattle creep above it.

Falling steeply, the line entered a deep cutting with concrete retaining walls; this marked the site of Barsham Tunnel which, according to the GER Magazine, was opened-out "a few years" before 1912. Beyond, trains crossed the River Stiffkey for a second time, and approached Walsingham with the little river flowing parallel to the right. For many travellers, this was perhaps the highlight of their journey; to the right, the so-called "Slipper Chapel" recalled the days when pilgrims would remove their shoes prior to walking barefoot for the final mile north to Walsingham. Walsingham station was only a short distance further on, and here, some 38 miles 58 chains from Norwich, the "Claud Hamilton" 4–4–0s brought their veteran panelled coaches to a stand beside a single platform on the up side of the line.

In Medieval times, Walsingham had been the most famous shrine in England, owing no doubt to a popular superstition (carefully fostered by local monks) that when Nazareth had fallen to the Moslems the Holy Virgin had abandoned the Sancta Casa there and taken up her abode at Walsingham. By the time of the Reformation, commercialism had become rampant, and Erasmus (who visited the shrine in 1511) recorded that he had been shown the milk of the Virgin – still in pristine condition! The shrine itself, he noted, was like "the seat of the gods, so bright and shining . . . with jewels, gold and silver". A few years later Henry VIII ordered the destruction of the monasteries and Walsingham sank back into a picturesque obscurity which lasted until 1931, when an Italian-style shrine was built as a centre of Anglican pilgrimage. Incongruous in Puritan East Anglia, the new shrine soon attracted large numbers of visitors, and with the revival of the Slipper Chapel as a Roman Catholic shrine, Walsingham once again became a major religious centre.

This sudden revival caught the LNER somewhat by surprise, for (unlike certain stations in the Catholic part of Ireland) Walsingham was by no means well-equipped to handle even occasional excursion traffic, and it lacked even a run-round loop. The facilities provided consisted of a single platform on the up side and five parallel goods sidings on the down side; the station was, however, a block post and it was theoretically possible (with the aid of some manoeuvring) for two goods trains or one goods and one passenger train to pass. When excursions were run, the usual practice was for the "Pilgrimage Specials" to set down at Walsingham and then run empty to Wells for turning and watering. The pilgrims, meanwhile, would visit either the Anglican or the Catholic shrine (perhaps both!) together with other places of historic or religious interest such as the Parish Church or the Priory ruins. In the late afternoon or early evening the excursion would return empty from Wells and pick up at Walsingham station or at "Slipper Chapel Halt". This last-named stopping place was in fact an occupation crossing near the Roman Catholic shrine; no platform was ever provided and passengers boarded their trains with the aid of portable steps.

Wighton Halt

Departing from Walsingham, northbound trains immediately glided across two level crossings and entered a cutting. Falling steadily, the railway emerged onto an embankment from which travellers could glimpse the River Stiffkey away to the east. Wighton, the last stop before Wells, was a simple, unstaffed halt with a short one-coach length platform on the up side. Its modest station buildings consisted of a tiny asbestos hut together with a cycle shed, and passengers wishing to embark or disembark here were requested to travel in the compartment nearest the guard.

Wells-next-the-Sea

Approaching its destination the railway followed the River Stiffkey down towards the sea. A short distance beyond Wighton the line passed within half a mile of a Celtic hill fort which was known erroneously as the "Danish Camp". Falling at 1 in 85 the route then curved north westwards for its final entry to Wells. An overbridge carried the B1105 road across the railway for the last time, and after a further half mile the A149 coast road crossed the line on the level.

With Wells now visible on the horizon, trains ran through a final short cutting, beyond which the harbour branch and the West Norfolk branch converged from the right and left respectively. Slowing to walking pace, the "Clauds" entered their terminus, and with the Heacham line running parallel to the left, finally came to a stand beneath the station's miniature overall roof. Here, 43 miles 21 chains from Norwich Thorpe, journeys came to an end. (There was a small ticket platform just outside the station, and when this facility was in use trains would pause briefly before drawing forward into the station proper.)

Wells station was a curious, old fashioned place which, throughout its life had two distinct parts. When first opened in 1857 the original line from Dereham had terminated in a single platform station, with a wooden overall roof and a combined engine shed-cum-goods shed to the north. Nine years later the opening of the West Norfolk branch from Heacham necessitated a modest enlargement, but instead of rebuilding their station the Great Eastern authorities allowed the West Norfolk company to erect a makeshift wooden platform beside the existing terminus. This second platform was an island, its outer face being used by Heacham services while the inner face flanked the Fakenham "main line" – giving travellers from Fakenham the option of alighting from either side of their train. (Although unusual, the resulting platform layout was not unique, and a similar arrangement could be found at Ventnor on the Isle of Wight Railway.)

Another unusual feature of Wells station concerned its run-round facilities – which were far too short for most passenger trains! There were, it is true, loops available beyond the limits of the passenger station, but in order to make use of them trains had to reverse out of the platforms and up the rising gradient towards Fakenham. Having backed their trains uphill it seemed sensible for train crews to let them return to the platforms with the aid of gravity, and what may have started as an unofficial expedient soon became the accepted mode of operation. When passengers had alighted, trains were backed out of the station and brought to a stand on the nearby gradient. The engine was then detached, and proceeded "light" to the engine shed for turning and servicing. Meanwhile the passenger vehicles were

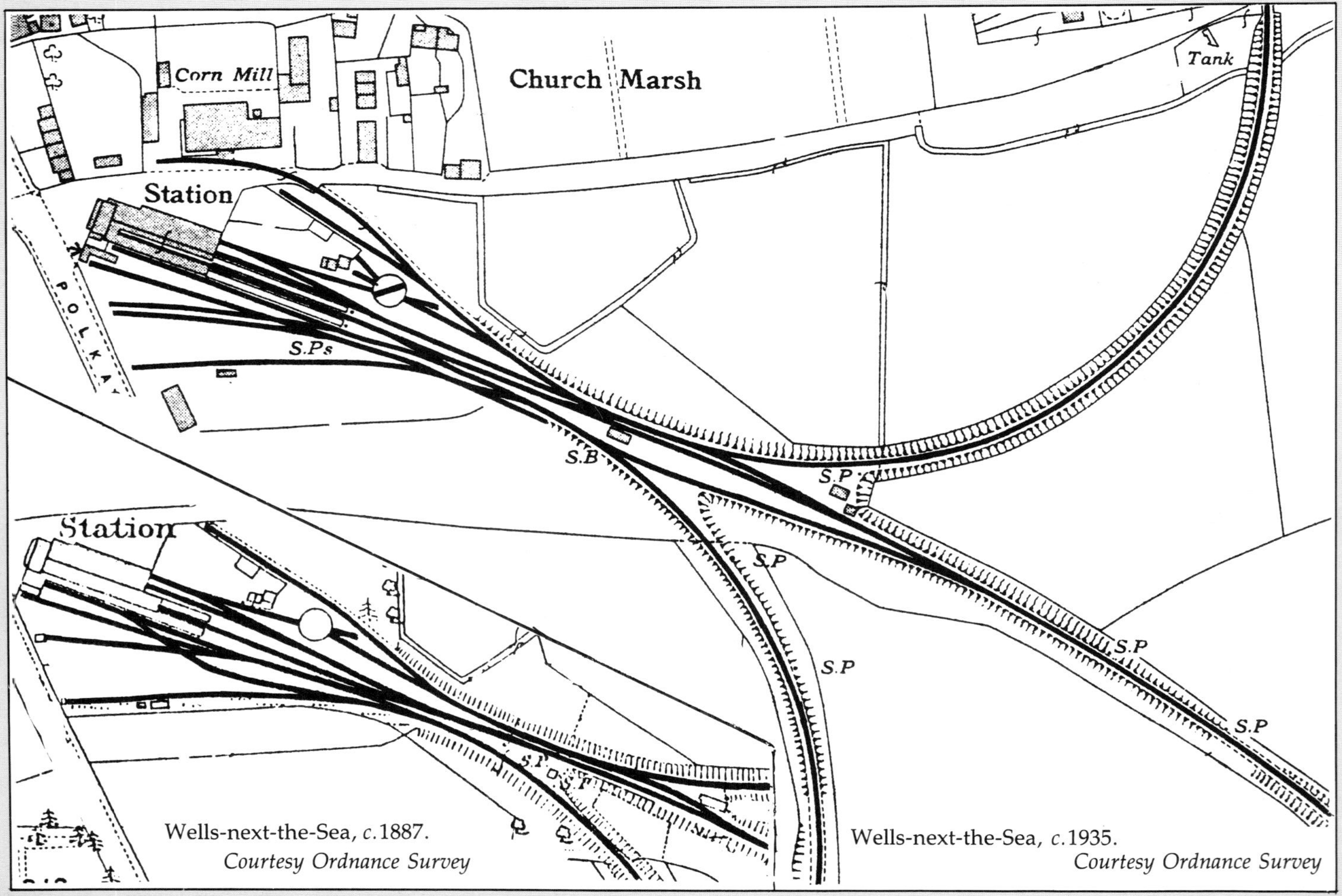

Wells-next-the-Sea, *c.*1887.
Courtesy Ordnance Survey

Wells-next-the-Sea, *c.*1935.
Courtesy Ordnance Survey

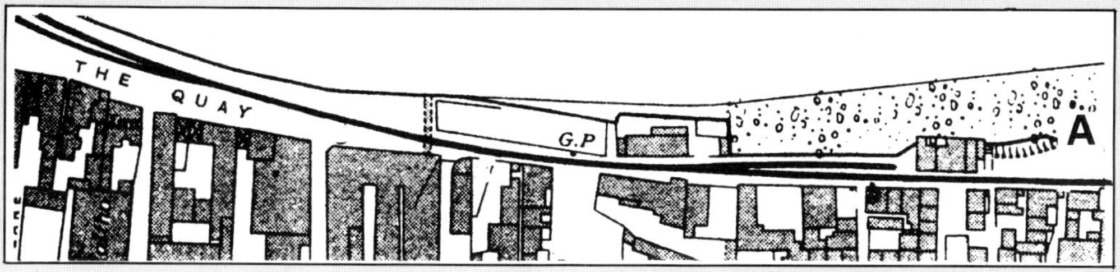

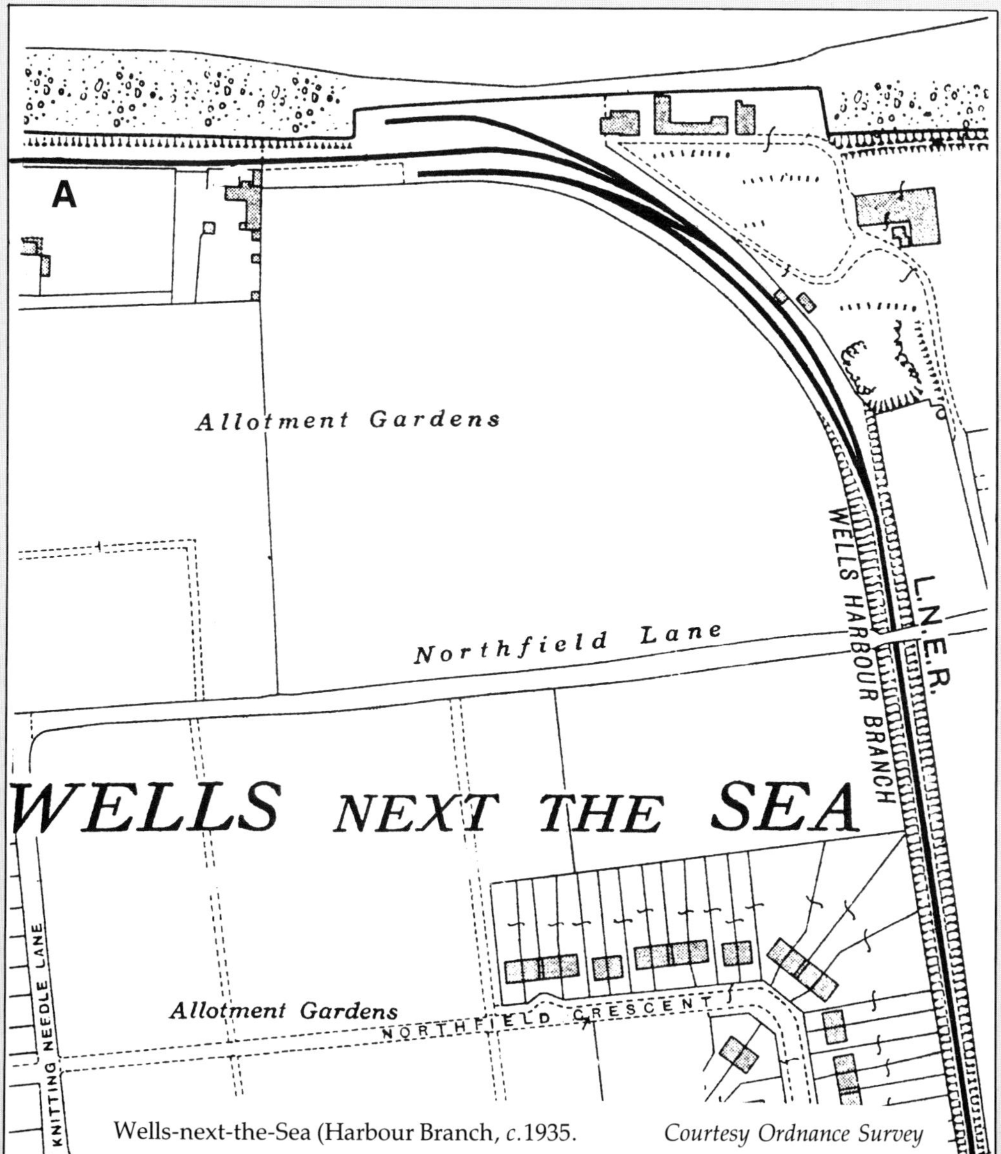

Wells-next-the-Sea (Harbour Branch, *c.*1935. *Courtesy Ordnance Survey*

allowed to roll down to the platforms under control from the guard's hand brake. (As a safety measure, trains were always marshalled with a guard's compartment at the Wells end of the train.) In 1931 a new connection was installed between the Fakenham and Heacham halves of the terminus, and this at last gave the station an adequate run-round facility.

The two platforms at Wells could accommodate only four-coach trains, and when longer formations had to be turned round, complicated manoeuvres were necessary – sometimes involving two engines if a spare one happened to be "on shed" at the appropriate time. Long trains did not appear with any regularity until the development of pilgrimage traffic in the 1930s – by which time the new loop was available. However, the new loop was of little use when long excursions arrived from the West Norfolk line, and on such occasions the trains had to be divided, reversed (in two operations) and then reunited before proceeding to Walsingham.

The main station buildings at Wells were "L" shaped, with one wing parallel to the platforms and the other extending at right angles behind the buffer stops. Of typical Great Eastern appearance, they were built of red brick with low-pitched "Georgian" style hipped roofs; internally, they contained a station master's house in addition to the usual booking office, waiting rooms and staff accommodation. Until the 1930s the adjoining train shed had covered only the Fakenham platform – Heacham passengers being left very much "out in the cold". A programme of improvements was belatedly carried out during the LNER period, and in its later days the station was provided with a modernised roof which extended horizontally across both platforms; an uncovered area was left directly above the track to facilitate smoke emission.

Goods facilities consisted of a small goods yard to the north of the passenger station, with four additional sidings to the south; one of the goods sidings gave access to Dewing & Kersley's nearby granary while others served coal wharves and a cattle dock. The goods shed, which adjoined the main terminal buildings, was most unusually sited in relation to the engine shed; in fact it occupied one end of the same building! The goods loading bay was situated behind the locomotive department, which meant that it could not be shunted when the loco shed was occupied – though as the latter was usually empty during the day, this was perhaps no problem. Nearby a 45 ft diameter turntable could accommodate 'E4s', 'D16s' and other small locomotive types, but *not* 'B12' 4–6–0s or other large engines. (On the rare occasions when such locomotives appeared they had to leave Wells tender-first.)

Other facilities at Wells included a water tower (with well beneath)

Dereham Central signal box was an enlarged Great Eastern standard cabin measuring approximately 48 ft x 12 ft. Situated to the south of the platforms, it controlled the main north-to-west curve which was used by Norwich to Kings Lynn services. *Edwin Wilmshurst*

A panoramic view of Dereham station, looking north towards Wells-next-the-Sea, with the main passenger buildings to the left and the large gabled goods shed to the right. *National Railway Museum*

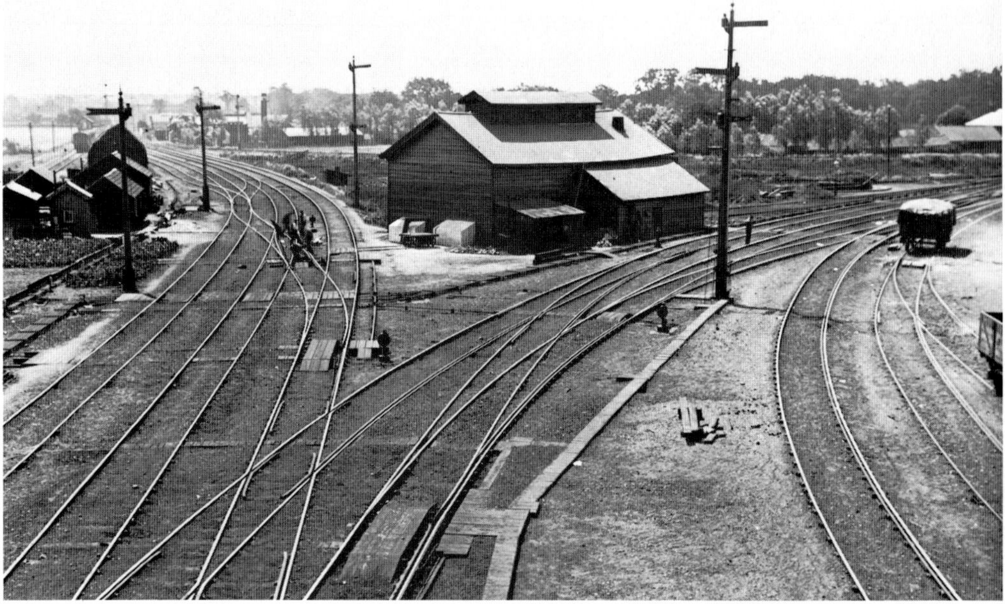

The original wooden engine shed at Dereham. This ramshackle structure was demolished around 1926 and a new shed of brick construction was erected in its place. The Norwich line can be seen to the left, while the north-to-west curve is visible to the right. *National Railway Museum*

Dereham West Junction, looking west, with London Road level crossing in the distance. The structure visible on the extreme right was a granary and the sidings seen to the left were part of the station's motive power depot; the date is around 1914. *National Railway Museum*

Dereham South Junction, looking south in Great Eastern days. The rail-served gas works can be glimpsed to the right, and Dereham South box is to the left of the picture. *National Railway Museum*

Another view of the two-road wooden engine shed at Dereham. A T26 (later E4) class 2–4–0 is standing on the north-to-west curve, and some of Dereham's extensive agricultural factories can be seen in the background. *National Railway Museum*

North Elmham station in July 1964 showing the austere modern-style building. *D. Thompson*

A general view of North Elmham station and dairy. *Lens of Sutton*

A group of boys from the Norfolk County School pose proudly for the camera in their naval-style uniform; the gentleman in sub Lieutenant's uniform (5th from left) is presumably the head master, while the GER staff on the extreme left are believed to be Mr Herod (*porter*) and Mr Paynter (*Station Master*) respectively. *A. Herod*

An Edwardian scene at County School station, looking north towards Wells with the Wroxham platform on the extreme right. *Alan R. Taylor*

The extensive maltings at Ryburgh, seen here in the Great Eastern period. Sadly this interesting early photograph does not show the original station buildings which were demolished after an air raid in World War Two.

Lens of Sutton

A post-war view of Ryburgh station and Mill; these buildings were damaged in an air raid, and although the mill was rebuilt the station building was merely a fragment of the original. *Lens of Sutton*

Ryburgh station with the surviving station buildings to the right.

Lens of Sutton

The Wells line ran on this three arch brick bridge above the River Wensum near Fakenham. *G.R Mortimer*

Fakenham station in the early 1960s, showing the single platform with its unusual canopy (the substantial brick wall probably supported an overall roof when the station was first opened). Fakenham station marked the northernmost limit of Norfolk Railway ownership – the Wells & Fakenham Railway commenced several chains beyond the level crossing. *Edwin Wilmshurst*

A general view of Walsingham station (facing Wells-next-the-Sea) on 18th May, 1959. *R.M. Casserley*

A general view of the single platform station at Walsingham looking south towards Wymondham, in the early 1960s. *C.L. Mowat Collection*

and a standard Great Eastern gabled wooden signal box which was sited at the convergence of the Fakenham and West Norfolk lines. The water column, which stood just a few feet away from the brick-built water tower, was a simple "fixed" type without a rotating horizontal arm; the flexible hose was attached to a simple, swan-necked pillar and the water flow was controlled by a raised wheel which projected vertically from the ground about 3 feet from the base of the column. A "fire devil" was provided for Winter use, and in true Great Eastern fashion this useful accessory was clipped upright beside the column.

In its heyday, Wells station gave employment to a considerable number of porters, clerks and signalmen, together with various other grades in the locomotive and permanent way departments. The station master, around 1904, was Mr Joseph Butters, and one of his immediate predecessors was Mr G. Paynter (presumably Gabriel Paynter who later served at County School). Later, in the years following World War I, the station master at Wells-next-the-Sea was Edward P. Friend.

Wells itself was an attractive coastal town, redolent of ships and the sea. Famous sailors associated with the area included Captain Marryat who lived at nearby Langham, Sir Cloudsley Shovel and Sir John Narborough – both of whom were born at Cockthorpe (4 miles to the west) – and Horatio Nelson, who was born at Burnham Thorpe in 1758. Later, during a long period of unemployment, Captain and Mrs Nelson returned to Norfolk, and during that bitter and frustrating period England's greatest naval hero is likely to have been a frequent visitor to Wells. (Later still, while Nelson was living with Lord and Lady Hamilton, Lady Nelson lived alone in the old Vicarage at Burnham Thorpe, with only the aging Rev. Edmund Nelson for company.)

Wells Harbour

The harbour branch, which diverged northwards near the station throat, was 69 chains in length and provided a useful link between Wells station and the busy quays on the opposite side of the town. Leaving the main line, this goods-only spur curved first north and then westwards in a great arc as it followed the approximate course of the original harbour channel. Reaching the quay it ran past a large grain mill and then terminated at the bottom of Staithe Street. From the holidaymaker's point of view, the presence of busy sidings on an otherwise picturesque quayside may have been an unwelcome intrusion, but in the days when all freight was moved by rail, these harbour sidings gave Wells a useful transport facility. In any case, Wells was not a seaside resort in the conventional sense – rather it was a working port and as such the harbour branch was an important part of what today might be termed the "local infrastructure".

Vessels seen in Wells harbour were, typically, coasters of up to 150 GRT carrying coal, cattle cake or grain. Spritsail barges and other small sailing vessels were a feature of the local scene until comparatively recent times – a regular visitor being the big 150 ton "Thames" Barge *Will Everard*; other barges seen at Wells included the *Zenobia, Scone, Cabby* and *Kindly Light,* while in earlier days, around 1900, the schooners *Cymric, Peggy, Patrician, Edith Crossfield* or *Mary Armstead* might have been seen tied-up alongside the quay. Methods of loading and unloading were primitive in the extreme, and Captain Jim Unglow* recalled unloading bags of cattle cake with the aid of the ship's own rigging and a winch; once the 16 or 18 stone bags were on the quayside they would be carried by gangs of labourers for a distance of some fifty yards – it could take three days to unload the entire hold!

The harbour branch was, technically, in two parts, and in their reports the Wells & Fakenham Directors usually distinguished between the *tramway* which actually ran along the quay, and a "goods branch" which connected it to the main line. It seems that construction of the latter was well advanced by 1857, but opening of the tramway was delayed by legal problems; the line was finally completed under an Act of 1859, though there is reason to believe that parts of the goods branch may have been in operation before this Act was obtained. The harbour line was worked on the "one-engine-in-steam" system, but (in later years at least) no train staff was needed. The line was little-used after World War II, and lifting took place in 1962.

At one point on its circuitous course between Wells Harbour and Wells station the harbour branch skirted a field used by local cricketers, and one amusing anecdote suggests that the "home" team would arrange for noisy shunting operations to take place at critical moments throughout important matches in the hope that sudden whistling and crashing of buffers would distract opposing batsmen! (This view was, of course, held by visiting players but denied by the Wells team.)

* Jim Unglow, MBE, *Sailorman* (1975) pp 112–15.

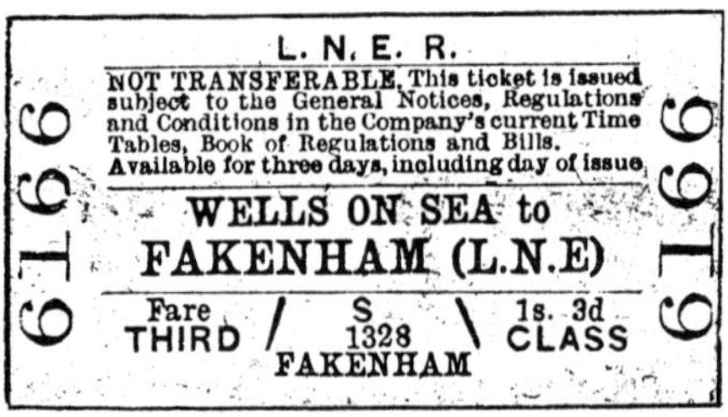
L. N. E. R.
NOT TRANSFERABLE. This ticket is issued subject to the General Notices, Regulations and Conditions in the Company's current Time Tables, Book of Regulations and Bills.
Available for three days, including day of issue.
WELLS ON SEA to
FAKENHAM (L.N.E)
Fare S 1s. 3d
THIRD 1328 CLASS
FAKENHAM
9169
9169

Chapter Six

The British Railways Era (1948–1982)

The immediate post-war era was a time of hope, in which the British people could look ahead to a brighter future with no poverty and no mass unemployment. Railwaymen in particular, anticipated that their newly-nationalised industry would receive long-overdue investment to replace locomotives and rolling stock – much of which still dated from the pre-grouping period.

Evidence of public ownership was provided by the application of bright new liveries – the red and cream colours applied to main line coaching stock being particularly attractive. Non-corridor vehicles received an overall LMS-type maroon livery (which was in effect a reversion to the final GER livery) while locomotives classified as "mixed traffic" engines were given L&NWR type lined black livery. When freshly applied these new colour schemes looked much brighter than the dreary black and brown of the LNER period – though in practice it took months, even years, before the older liveries were replaced.

Locomotives and Rolling Stock in the BR Era

Apart from these new liveries, the BR era produced few immediate changes, and the Wells branch still looked much the same as it had done in Great Eastern days. Although Norwich retained some 'E4' 2–4–0s, "Claud Hamilton" 4–4–0s had virtually assumed command of branch passenger services, while freight workings were handled by 'J15s', 'J17s', 'J19s' or even 'N7' 0–6–2Ts. Other types occasionally appeared, including 'B12' 4–6–0s and ex-LMS Ivatt '4MT' 2–6–0s, which worked through to Walsingham with "Pilgrim Specials" – sometimes taking the West Norfolk route via Heacham and Burnham Market.

Coaching stock also retained a predominantly pre-grouping flavour, and Norwich–Wells services were invariably composed of antiquated, gas-lit vehicles from the former GER, GNR, GCR or NER companies; more modern LNER vehicles also appeared, but as these Gresley-designed coaches were of Great Northern design their comparative modernity was by no means apparent to ordinary travellers! (A summary of locomotive classes seen on the Wells branch is given in **Table 4**.)

Post-war train services were, in effect, merely a continuation of the basic pattern established in the GER period. In 1950 for example there were six trains each way daily, taking around two hours for the 43¼ mile journey. Extra services ran on Saturdays including a short-distance Wells–Dereham working; the Sunday service provided two trains each way, with additional workings in the Summer months.

Table 4
PRINCIPAL LOCOMOTIVE CLASSES USED ON THE WELLS BRANCH 1900–1969

GER Class	*Wheelbase*	*LNE/BR Class*	*Notes*
No. 1	2–4–0	–	Worked most services until about 1912.
T26	2–4–0	E4	Became standard motive power on both the Wells–Norwich and Wells–Heacham lines from 1912 until the later 1930s.
Y14	0–6–0	J15	Worked on goods services during the 20th Century.
T19	4–4–0	D13	Built as 2–4–0s, many of these engines were later given a leading bogie in which form they were designated 'D13s' by the LNER; while not as characteristic as the 'E4s', they occasionally worked on the branch in the 1920s and 1930s.
Claud Hamilton	4–4–0	D15 D16/2 D16/3	Gradually assumed command of branch passenger services in the late 1930s, supplementing and then finally superseding the 'E4s'. Thereafter these ex-main line engines remained standard motive power until dieselisation in 1955.
	0–6–0	J17	Worked freight traffic from the 1930s until replaced by diesels.
	0–6–0	J19	Less common than the earlier 0–6–0s, these Gresley rebuilds first appeared in the 1930s and lasted until the BR era.
	2–4–2T	F3	Often worked the Tuesday-only through coaches from Liverpool Street to Wells via Forncett and Wymondham.
1000	0–6–2T	N7	These former suburban tanks appeared in East Anglia in the 1950s, and worked freight (possibly some passenger) services on the Wells branch.
1500	4–6–0	B12	Worked some excursion traffic to Walsingham, but were hardly ideal types for use on the branch as they were too big for the turntable at Wells!

–	2–6–0	4MT	Ex-LMS Ivatt 2–6–0s occasionally worked on "Pilgrimage Specials".
–	4–4–0	D2	These former GNR engines worked some services before and during the Second World War.
–	A1A–A1A	31	Class 31s worked excursion traffic to Walsingham and also freight services, eventually becoming the usual motive power on surviving freight workings to Ryburgh and Fakenham.
–	Bo-Bo	15	Class 15s occasionally worked on Walsingham excursions, coupled in pairs, and they also appeared on local freight services.

There were still, in the early 1950s, two freight workings each way, but this was later reduced to just one (except during the busy sugar beet season). The West Norfolk branch had a slightly improved service with five trains each way, rising to six on Mondays, Wednesdays and Saturdays. Fares were in the 1950s remarkably cheap and a single ticket from Liverpool Street to Wells cost the prospective traveller only 22*s.* 9*d.* (i.e. £1.15)!

With petrol rationing in force, and private road hauliers restricted by government legislation, the Wells to Norwich line remained relatively busy throughout the late 1940s and early 1950s. The neighbouring Hunstanton and Cromer lines, on the other hand, were enjoying a massive revival as holidaymakers – eager to experience the freedom of civilian life after six years of total war – flocked to the seaside in increasing numbers. Sadly, the West Norfolk branch failed to experience a comparable post-war boom, and on 31st May, 1952 the Wells to Heacham passenger service was withdrawn.

Freight and excursion traffic continued to run via Heacham, and on 29th June 'B12' 4–6–0 No. 61533 traversed the route with a Kettering to Walsingham "Pilgrimage Special". At Wells the long train was divided, and the 'B12' continued into the station with the front portion; there, a "Claud" 4–4–0 backed on to the rear of the divided train, bringing it out of the terminus and onto the Dereham line. The operation was then repeated with the rear half of the excursion, and in this way the train was transferred from the West Norfolk branch to the Dereham "main line". These complicated manoeuvres were repeated in the evening and, having regained the West Norfolk line, No. 61533 set off for Heacham – running tender first as it was too big to fit on the Wells turntable! In the event, this was the last passenger

Table 45 NORWICH, DEREHAM, KING'S LYNN and WELLS-ON-SEA

Second class only between Norwich and King's Lynn and Wells-on-Sea except where otherwise shown

Miles		Week Days																				
		am	am	am	am		am	am	am	am	am	am	am	am		pm	pm	pm	pm ¶	pm	pm	pm
—	**Norwich** (Thorpe) ... dep	..	..	6 35	..	..	7 48	..	..	9 21	1030	..	1039	..	..	12 5	12 11	..	..	1 8	..	2 10
6¼	Hethersett	..	..	..	..	..	..	..	..	..	..	..	1050	..	..	..	..	..	..	1 19	..	2 21
10¾	**Wymondham** ... arr	..	..	6 50	..	..	8 6	..	..	9 36	1048	..	1056	..	..	1219	12 25	..	..	1 25	..	2 27
—	6 **London** (L'pool St) 5 dep	..	..	..	..	..	..	4 24	..	4A35	..	6 51	6e54	..	..	9A30	9B47	..		10P30	..	10V30
—	**Wymondham** .. .. dep	..	..	6 51	..	..	..	8 13	..	9 37	..	1057	1057	..	..	1220	12 28	..	Saturdays only	1 28	..	2 28
14	Kimberley Park	..	..	6 57	..	..	..	8 19	..	9 43	..	11 3	11 3	..	..	1226	12 34	..		1 34	..	2 34
15½	Hardingham	..	..	7 1	..	..	..	8 24	..	9 48	..	11 8	11 8	..	..	1231	12 39	..		1 39	..	2 39
17½	Thuxton	..	..	7 5	..	..	..	8 28	..	9 52	..	1112	1112	..	..	1235	12 43	..		1 43	..	2 43
19¾	Yaxham	..	..	7 11	..	..	..	8 34	..	9 58	..	1118	1118	..	..	1241	12 49	..		1 49	..	2 49
21½	**Dereham** ... arr	..	..	7 15	..	..	..	8 38	..	10 2	..	1122	1122	..	..	1245	12 53	..		1 53	..	2 53
—	**Dereham** .. .. dep	..	6 47	..	8 6	..	..	..	8 46	..	..	..	..	1127	..	..	..	1 1	..	..	2 12	3 2
25¼	Wendling	..	6 55	..	8 14	..	..	..	8 53	..	..			1135	..			1 9	..	..	2 20	3 10
28¼	Fransham	..	7 1	..	8 20	..	..	..	8 59	..	..			1141	..			1 15	..	..	2 26	3 16
29¾	Dunham	..	7 5	..	8 24	..	..	..	9 3	..	..			1145	..			1 19	..	..	2 30	3 20
33¾	**Swaffham**	..	7U17	..	8 31	..	..	..	9 10	..	..	Saturdays only	Except Saturdays	1152	..	Except Saturdays	Saturdays only	1 25	1 35	..	2 38	3 28
39¼	Narborough & Pentney	..	7 26	..	8 40	..	..	..	9 22	..	..			12 5	..			..	1 47	..	2 47	3 37
43	East Winch	..	7 33	..	8 47	..	..	..	9 29	..	..			1212	..			..	1 55	..	2 54	3 44
45	Middleton Towers	..	7 38	..	8 52	..	..	..	9 34	..	..			1217	..			..	2 0	..	2 59	3 49
48½	**King's Lynn** .. arr	..	7 43	..	8 58	..	..	..	9 41	..	..	..	..	1224	..	..	..	..	2 8	..	3 6	3 58
89½	43 Cambridge ... arr	..	9 56	..	10C 7	..	..	..	12H7	..	..	..	..	2 45	..	..	..	..	3J50	..	4L39	6D50
145½	43 London (L'pool St) ,,	..	1121	..	11C28	..	..	..	1Y37	..	..	..	..	4 52	..	..	..	..	5J12	..	6L 2	..
—	**Dereham** ... dep	6 4	..	7 17	..	..	..	8 54	..	10 6	..	1123	1124	..	..	1254	12 54	..	..	2 3	..	..
26¼	North Elmham	6 13	..	7 26	..	..	..	9 3	..	1015	..	1131	1132	..	..	1 3	1 3	..	..	2 11	..	..
27¾	County School	6 17	..	7 30	..	..	..	9 7	..	1022	..	1136	1136	..	..	1 7	1 7	..	..	2 18	..	..
31¼	Ryburgh	6 24	..	7 37	..	..	..	9 14	..	1029	..	1141	1142	..	..	1 14	1 14	..	..	2 25	..	..
33¾	**Fakenham** (East)	6 29	..	7 43	..	..	..	9 19	..	1034	..	1146	1147	..	..	1 19	1 19	..	..	2 30	..	..
38¾	Walsingham	6 38	..	7 52	..	..	..	9 28	..	1043	..	1154	1155	..	..	1 28	1 28	..	..	2 39	..	..
40¼	Wighton Halt	..	..	7 57	..	..	..	9 33	..	1048	..	1158	1159	..	..	1 33	1 33	..	..	2 44	..	..
43¼	**Wells-on-Sea** .. .. arr	6 47	..	8 3	..	..	..	9 39	..	1054	..	12 4	12 5	..	..	1 39	1 39	..	..	2 50	..	..

	Week Days—continued																Sundays					
	pm	pm	pm	pm	pm	pm	pm	pm	pm	pm	pm		pm	pm	pm		am	am	pm	pm	pm	
Norwich (Thorpe) ... dep	3 5	3 22	..	..	4 56	5 35	..	6 10	6 20	..	..	..	8 56	9 32	..	..	9 51	..	..	5 45	8 15	..
Hethersett	3 16	3 33	..	..	5 8	..	..	6 21	6 31	..	..	..	..	9 42	..	..	10 2	..	..	..	8 26	..
Wymondham ... arr	3 23	3 40	..	..	5 15	5 50	..	6 28	6 38	..	..	..	9 11	9 48	..	..	10 9	..	..	6 0	8 33	..
6 **London** (L'pool St) 5 dep	12A30	12A30	..	..	1A30	3G30	..	3A30	..	..	..	..	6K30	6K30		..	..	..	..	2 24	..	..
Wymondham .. .. dep	3 26	3 41	..	..	5 16	5 51	..	6 29	6 39	..	..	..	9 12	9 49	Saturdays only	..	1010	..	..	6 1	8 34	..
Kimberley Park	3 32	3 47	..	..	5 22	5 57	..	6 35	6 45	..	..	..	9 18	9 55		..	1016	..	..	6 7	8 40	..
Hardingham	3 37	3 52	..	..	5 27	6 2	..	6 40	6 50	..	..	..	9 23	10 0		..	1021	..	..	6 12	8 45	..
Thuxton	3 41	3 56	..	..	5 31	6 6	..	6 44	6 54	..	..	..	9 27	10 4		..	1025	..	..	6 16	8 49	..
Yaxham	3 47	4 2	..	..	5 37	6 12	..	6 50	7 0	..	..	..	9 33	1010		..	1031	..	..	6 22	8 55	..
Dereham ... arr	3 51	4 6	..	..	5 41	6 16	..	6 54	7 4	..	..	..	9 37	1014		..	1035	..	..	6 26	8 59	..
Dereham .. .. dep			4 17	5 14	..	..	6 18			7 18	8 19	..	9 43		1018	..	..	..	..	..		..
Wendling			4 25	5 22	..	..	6 26			7 26	8 27	..	9 51		1026	..	..	..	..	..		..
Fransham			4 31	5 28	..	..	6 32			7 32	8 33	..	9 57		1032	..	..	..	..	..		..
Dunham			4 35	5 32	..	..	6 36			7 36	8 37	..	10 1		1036	..	..	..	..	..		..
Swaffham	Except Saturdays	Saturdays only	4 42	5d43	..	..	6 44	Saturdays only	Except Saturdays	7d47	8d48	..	10 9	Saturdays only	1044	..	..	..	..	..	From Yarmouth (Vauxhall) dep 7 33 pm (Table 48)	..
Narborough & Pentney			4 52	5 52	..	..	6 54			7 56	8 57	..	1019		1054	..	..	..	..	..		..
East Winch			4 59	5 59	..	..	7 2			8 3	9 4	..	1026		11 1	..	..	..	..	..		..
Middleton Towers			5 4	6 4	..	..	7 7			8 8	9 9	..	1031		11 6	..	..	..	..	..		..
King's Lynn .. arr			5 10	6 10	..	..	7 14			8 14	9 15	..	1038		1113	..	..	..	..	..		..
43 Cambridge ... arr	..	..	7 7	7N32	..	..	8R36	..	..	..	12F46	..		..	..	..	..	..	..	..		..
43 London (L'pool St) ,,	..	..	8 40	11Q23	..	..	9T58	..	..	..	a2F23	..		..	..	..	..	..	..	..		..
Dereham ... dep	4 15	4 15	..	..	5 42	..	..	7 12	7 12	..	..	..		1016	..	..	1037	1047	1 20	6 30		..
North Elmham	4 24	4 24	..	..	5 50	..	..	7 21	7 21	..	..	..		1025	..	..	..	1056	1 29	6 39		..
County School	4 28	4 28	..	..	5 57	..	..	7 25	7 25	..	..	..		1029	..	..	..	11 1	1 33	6 46		..
Ryburgh	4 35	4 35	..	..	6 4	..	..	7 32	7 32	..	..	..	Except Saturdays	1036	..	..	..	11 8	1 40	6 53		..
Fakenham (East)	4 40	4 40	..	..	6 9	..	..	7 37	7 37	..	..	..		1041	..	..	..	1113	1 46	6 58		..
Walsingham	4 49	4 49	..	..	6 18	..	..	7 49	7 49	..	..	..		1050	..	..	11 7	1122	1 55	7 7		..
Wighton Halt	4 54	4 54	..	..	6 23	..	..	7 54	7 54	..	..	..		1055	..	..	..	1127	2 0	7 12		..
Wells-on-Sea .. arr	5 0	5 0	..	..	6 29	..	..	8 0	8 0	..	..	..		11 1	..	..	1116	1133	2 6	7 18	..	..

¶ First and Second class
A Via Norwich (Thorpe)
a am
B On 16th June, 8th and 15th September departs Liverpool Street 9 30 am via Norwich
C Fridays and Saturdays only. Runs 30th June to 8th September inclusive
D Via March and St. Ives
d Arrives 4 minutes *earlier*
E Except Saturdays
e Via Norwich (Thorpe). Second class only Ipswich to Norwich
F Via March. On Saturday nights via Downham
G Via Norwich. On Saturdays departs Liverpool Street 2 24 pm via Ely
H On Fridays and Saturdays 29th June to 8th September inclusive arrives Cambridge 12 18 pm
J Saturdays only. Runs 14th July to 1st September inclusive
K Via Norwich (Thorpe). The East Anglian. Limited accommodation
L On Fridays and Saturdays 7th July to 1st September inclusive arrives Cambridge 4 48 pm and Liverpool Street 6 10 (6 13 pm on Saturdays)
N Not after 8th September. On Saturdays arrives Cambridge 7 40 pm. Also runs on Wednesday 12th and Saturday 15th September Cambridge arrive 9 16 pm via St. Ives
P Saturdays only. Via Norwich (Thorpe)
Q Runs Mondays to Fridays until 6th July and from 3rd to 7th September. Also runs every Saturday until 8th September Liverpool St. arr 9 53 pm
R Mondays to Fridays. Runs 9th July to 31st August inclusive. Also runs on Saturdays 28th July to 1st September inclusive Cambridge arrive 9 18 pm
S Saturdays only
T Except Saturdays. Runs 9th July to 31st August inclusive
U Arrives 5 minutes *earlier*
V Except Sats. Via Norwich (Thorpe)
Y On Fridays and Saturdays 29th June to 8th September inclusive arrives Liverpool St. 1 42 pm and on Saturdays 16th, 23rd June & 15th Sept. 1 33 pm

For OTHER TRAINS between Norwich and Wymondham, see Table 6

Passenger Timetable for 1956.

Table 45—*continued* WELLS-ON-SEA, KING'S LYNN, DEREHAM, and NORWICH

Second class only between Wells-on-Sea and King's Lynn and Norwich except where otherwise shown

Miles	Mls	Week Days	am		am	am		am	am		am		am	am		am	am	am ¶	pm	pm	pm	pm	pm
—		**Wells-on-Sea** .. .. dep	..	..	..	6 55	..	..	8 8	..	..	..	..	9 49	..	11 2	11 2	Saturdays only	From Thetford dep 11E31 am (Table 37) 11S38 am	1210	1234	..	1 44
2¾		Wighton Halt	....	....	....	7 1	....	....	8 14	....	....	....	....	9 55	....	11 8	11 8			1216	1240	....	1 50
4½		Walsingham	..	..	..	7 6	..	..	8 19	..	..	..	..	10 0	..	11 13	11 13			1221	1245	..	1 55
9½		**Fakenham** (East)	....	....	....	7 16	....	....	8 29	....	....	....	....	1010	....	11 23	11 23			1230	1254	....	2 5
12		Ryburgh	..	..	..	7 21	..	..	8 34	..	..	..	..	1015	..	11 28	11 28			1235	1259	..	2 10
15½		County School	....	....	....	7 32	....	....	8 40	....	....	....	....	1021	....	11 37	11 37			1241	1 8	....	2 17
17		North Elmham	..	..	..	7 36	..	..	8 44	..	..	..	..	1025	..	11 41	11 41			1245	1 12	..	2 21
21½		**Dereham** arr	....	....	....	7 44	....	....	8 52	....	....	....	....	1033	....	11 49	11 49			1252	1 19	....	2 28
—		43 **London** (L St) dep	..	..	..	..	..	..	..	..	..	..	5 54	..	..	..	..	8C27		..	..	8R24	..
—		43 Cambridge ... ,,	....	....	....	....	....	....	....	....	....	....	8H 2	....	....	....	....	10C 3		....	....	10T15	....
—	—	**King's Lynn** .. dep	..	..	6 48	..	..	7 48	..	..	9 3	..	9 52	..	..	Except Saturdays	Saturdays only	11 42		Except Saturdays	Saturdays only	1 5	..
—	3¼	Middleton Towers	....	....	6 54	....	....	7 54	....	....	9 9	....	9 58	....	....			11 49				1 12	....
—	5¼	East Winch	..	..	6 59	..	..	7 59	..	..	9 14	..	10 3	..	..			11 55				1 17	..
—	8¾	Narborough & Pentney	....	....	7 6	....	....	8 6	....	....	9 21	....	1010	....	....			12 3	....			1 24	....
—	14¼	**Swaffham**	..	..	7h20	..	..	8 15	..	..	9 30	..	1019	..	..			12 15	1225			1 34	..
—	18¼	Dunham	....	....	7 28	....	....	8 25	....	....	9 37	....	1026	....	....			....	1233			1 42	....
—	19¾	Fransham	..	..	7 32	..	..	8 29	..	..	..	..	1030	..	..			..	1237			1 46	..
—	22½	Wendling	....	....	7 38	....	....	8 35	....	....	9 45	....	1036	....	....			....	1243			1 52	....
—	26½	**Dereham** .. .. arr	..	..	7 45	..	..	8 41	..	..	9 51	..	1043	..	..			..	1250			1 59	..
—		**Dereham** dep	6 50	....	....	7 50	....	....	8 58	....	9 56	....	....	1047	....	11 50	11 54	..	....	1253	1 20	....	2 29
23½		Yaxham	6 54	..	..	7 55	..	..	9 3	..	..	..	..	1051	..	11 54	11 58	..	..	1257	1 24	..	2 33
26		Thuxton	7 0	....	....	8 1	....	....	9 9	....	....	....	....	1057	....	12 0	12 4	....	....	1 3	1 30	....	2 39
27½		Hardingham	7 4	..	..	8 5	..	..	9 13	..	..	..	..	11 1	..	12 4	12 8	..	..	1 7	1 34	..	2 43
29¼		Kimberley Park	7 8	....	....	8 9	....	....	9 17	....	....	....	....	11 5	....	12 9	12 12	....	....	1 11	1 38	....	2 47
33		**Wymondham** .. .. arr	7 13	..	..	8 14	..	..	9 22	..	1014	..	..	1110	..	12 13	12 17	..	..	1 16	1 43	..	2 52
146¾		6 **London** (L'pool St) 5 arr	10A0	....	....	1121	....	....	12J35	....	1V37	....	....	1K55	....	3A30	3A30	....	....	4A34	5 0	....	6A39
—		**Wymondham** dep	7 14	..	..	8 16	..	..	9 24	..	1015	..	..	1112	..	12 15	12 19	..	..	1 17	1 44	..	2 53
37		Hethersett	....	....	....	8 24	....	....	....	....	....	....	....	1120	....	....	....	....	....	....	1 52	....	3 1
43½		**Norwich** (Thorpe) .... arr	7 31	..	..	8 34	..	..	9 39	..	1028	..	..	1130	..	12 29	12 37	..	..	1 31	2 3	..	3 10

	Week Days—*continued*																Sundays					
	pm	pm	pm	pm	pm		pm	pm	pm	pm	pm	pm	pm	pm			am	am	pm	pm	pm	
Wells-on-Sea .. .. dep	..	3 15	..	..	5 24	..	..	..	7 18	..	8 18	Saturdays only	Except Saturday	11 6	..	..	..	1145	4 0	6 12	7 26	..
Wighton Halt	....	3 21	....	....	5 30	....	....	....	7 24	....	8 24			1112	....	....	....	1151	4 6	6 18	....	....
Walsingham	..	3 26	..	..	5 35	..	..	..	7 29	..	8 29			1117	..	..	..	1156	4 11	6 23	7 36	..
Fakenham (East)	....	3 36	....	....	5 45	....	....	....	7d42	....	8 39			1127	....	....	....	12 7	4 21	6 34	....	....
Ryburgh	..	3 41	..	..	5 50	..	..	..	7 47	..	8 45			1132	..	..	..	1212	4 26	6 39	..	..
County School	....	3 47	....	....	5 56	....	....	....	7 53	....	8 51			1138	....	....	....	1218	4 33	6 45	....	....
North Elmham	..	3 51	..	..	6 0	..	..	..	7 57	..	8 55			1142	..	..	..	1222	4 37	6 49	..	..
Dereham arr	....	3 59	....	....	6 8	....	....	....	8 5	....	9 3			1150	....	....	....	1230	4 45	6 57	8 4	....
43 **London** (L St.) dep	12B24	..	..	12S27	..	..	2U24	4G30	..	..	..	5 54	5 54		..	..	To Yarmouth (Vauxhall) arr 11 2 am (Table 48)	..	..	..	..	..
43 Cambridge ... ,,	1B49	....	1D53	2 35	....	....	3U56	5G46	....	....	....	7 22	7 27		....	....		....	....	....	....	....
King's Lynn .. dep	3 14	..	4 8	5 15	..	..	6 15	7 19	..	8 19	..	9 20	9 20	Saturdays only	..	..		..	..	..	..	..
Middleton Towers	3 21	....	4 15	5 21	....	....	6 21	7 25	....	8 26	....	9 26	9 26		....	....		....	....	....	....	....
East Winch	3 26	..	4 20	5 26	..	..	6 26	7 30	..	8 31	..	9 31	9 31		..	..		..	..	..	..	..
Narborough & Pentney	3 38	....	4 31	5 33	....	....	6 33	7 37	....	8 38	....	9 38	9 38		....	....		....	....	....	....	....
Swaffham	3 48	..	4d43	5 42	..	..	6d45	7 46	..	8 47	..	9k51	9k51		..	..		..	..	..	..	..
Dunham	3 56	....	4 51	5 49	....	....	6 52	7 53	....	8 54	....	9 58	10d2	....	....	....		....	....	....	....	....
Fransham	4 0	..	4 55	5 53	..	..	6 56	7 56	..	8 58	..	10 1	10 6	..	..	..		..	..	..	..	..
Wendling	4 6	....	5 1	5 59	....	....	7 2	8 2	....	9 4	....	10 7	1012	....	....	....		....	....	....	....	....
Dereham .. .. arr	4 12	..	5 8	6 6	..	..	7 9	8 9	..	9 11	..	1013	1019	..	..	..		..	..	..	..	..
Dereham dep	....	4 16	....	....	6 10	....	....	....	8 12	....	9 15	....	....	....	....	....	9 38	....	4 47	6 59	8 6	....
Yaxham	..	4 20	..	..	6 14	..	..	..	8 16	..	9 19	..	..	..	..	..	9 42	..	4 51	7 3	8 10	..
Thuxton	....	4 26	....	....	6 20	....	....	....	8 22	....	9 25	....	....	....	....	....	9 48	....	4 57	7 9	8 16	....
Hardingham	..	4 30	..	..	6 24	..	..	..	8 26	..	9 29	..	..	..	..	..	9 52	..	5 1	7 13	8 20	..
Kimberley Park	....	4 34	....	....	6 28	....	....	....	8 30	....	9 33	....	....	....	....	....	9 56	....	5 5	7 17	8 24	....
Wymondham .. .. arr	..	4 39	..	..	6 33	..	..	..	8 35	..	9 38	..	..	..	..	..	10 1	..	5 10	7 22	8 29	..
6 **London** (L'pool St) 5 arr	....	7N55	....	....	11Q56	....	....	....	....	....	2a23	....	....	....	....	....	1A 4	....	8 19	12A14	2a18	....
Wymondham dep	..	4 44	..	..	6 35	..	..	..	8 36	..	9 39	..	..	..	..	..	10 3	..	5 12	7 24	8 31	..
Hethersett	....	4 52	....	....	6 43	....	....	....	....	....	....	....	....	....	....	....	1011	....	....	7 32	8 39	....
Norwich (Thorpe) .... arr	..	5 4	..	..	6 56	..	..	..	8 49	..	9 52	..	..	..	..	..	1020	..	5 27	7 41	8 48	..

¶ First and Second class
A Via Norwich (Thorpe)
a am
B On Saturdays departs Liverpool Street 12 14 and Cambridge 1 47 pm (12 10 and 1 35 pm respectively on 16th, 23rd June and 15th September)
C On 8th and 15th September departs Liverpool Street 8 24 and Cambridge 9 53 am
D Via St. Ives and March
d Arrives 4 minutes *earlier*
E Except Saturdays
G On Saturdays departs Liverpool Street 4 27 and Cambridge 5 56 pm
H From 23rd July to 1st September inclusive departs Cambridge 8 37 pm
h Arrives 6 minutes *earlier*
J Via Norwich (Thorpe) On Saturdays arrives Liverpool St. 12 45 pm
K Via Norwich (Thorpe). The East Anglian. Limited accommodation On Fridays and Saturdays arrives Liverpool Street 2 6 pm
k Arr 5 minutes *earlier*
N Via Norwich (Thorpe). On Saturdays arrives Liverpool Street 8 6 pm
Q Via Norwich (Thorpe). On Saturdays arrives Liverpool St. 9 53 pm via Ely
R Mondays to Fridays. Also Runs Saturdays 14th July to 25th August Liverpool Street departs 9 50 am
S Saturdays only
T Via St. Ives and March. On Saturdays 14th July to 25th August departs Cambridge 11 14 am via Ely
U On Fridays and Saturdays 29th June to 8th September departs Liverpool Street 2 27 and Cambridge 4 9 pm
V On Saturdays arrives Liverpool Street 1 33 pm (1 21 pm via Norwich (Thorpe))

For OTHER TRAINS between Wymondham and Norwich, see Table 6

train to run through from Wells to Heacham. The West Norfolk branch was not the only line closed at this relatively early date, and on 13th September, 1952 all passenger services were withdrawn from the East Norfolk branch between Wroxham and County School.

The East Coast Floods

The late Summer of 1952 had been unusually wet, and on the night of 15th–16th August the Devon village of Lynmouth was wrecked by a devastating flash flood. This major disaster was still fresh in the public mind when, on the night of 31st January, 1953 the low-lying eastern counties suffered an immeasurably greater catastrophe. On that day a deep depression moved south from Iceland producing gale force winds which coincided with a high flood tide – the result being a tidal surge that breached protective dykes throughout East Anglia. Coastal villages were flooded to a depth of up to 6 ft, while at Wells the inundating waters swept along the harbour branch, and (following the course of the original harbour channel) poured into the station, flooding its platforms and sidings. Between Wells and Burnham Market the angry seas scattered sleepers and ballast in all directions and effectively severed the West Norfolk branch. At Blakeney, the famous nature reserve on Blakeney Point was submerged, and the sea flowed inland for two miles. At Hunstanton, meanwhile, a train had attempted to reach Kings Lynn – but came to a stand near Heacham when the rising waters extinguished its fire.

Dawn, on the 1st February, 1952, revealed a picture of utter devastation, and it seemed that centuries of land reclamation work had been undone in a matter of hours. Dykes were broken, dunes partially dispersed, and thousands of specially-planted pine trees had been destroyed. Over thirty people had been drowned north of Heacham, and there had been several more local fatalities at Salthouse (a few miles along the coast from Wells). A curious feature of the flood damage was the way in which, for mile after mile, telegraph poles were left leaning at the same drunken angle. Damage to the West Norfolk branch was so severe that BR did not consider that the Wells to Burnham Market section was worth reinstating, and this portion of the route was therefore closed (though a few goods trains later traversed parts of the damaged line in connection with flood repair work on the surrounding farmland). At Holkham, a marker was placed on the former station building to show how high the waters had risen.

Dieselisation

In September 1955 BR introduced a fleet of brand new diesel mul-

Wighton Halt seen here in July 1964. *D. Thompson*

Class D13 4–4–0 No. 8030 enters Wells-next-the-Sea on 29th June 1936; note the assorted coaching stock and the Heacham branch going to right of the signal cabin. *H.C. Casserley*

Two views of Claud Hamilton 4–4–0 No. 62564 at Wells-next-the-Sea on 1st September, 1955. *H.C. Casserley*

The 5.54 pm train for Norwich at Wells-next-the-Sea on 29th June 1936. The first carriage is a 48 ft 3 in. x 8 ft 6 in. lavatory composite with luggage compartment at the far end (these were built in 1900–06 and most lasted to BR days; the last was withdrawn in 1955). *H.C. Casserley*

A post-closure view of the terminal buildings at Wells-next-the-Sea; although built by the Wells & Fakenham Railway, these buildings were not unlike the Great Eastern's standard "1860s" style stations. *Lens of Sutton*

A general view of the approaches to Wells-next-the-Sea; the loop line seen disappearing behind the GER style signal box was added in LNER days.
C.L. Mowat Collection

Wells-next-the-Sea, photographed in the 1930s after the station had lost its original overall roof. The combined engine shed/goods shed can be seen to the right; class E4 2–4–0 No. 7415 visits in the platform with an afternoon train.
H.C. Casserley

Wells-next-the-Sea on 31st May 1952. An ex-Great Eastern 0–6–0 stands in the West Norfolk platform, while a Claud Hamilton 4–4–0 simmers outside the engine shed. *H.B. Priestley*

A "full house" at Wells on 15th June 1952, with "Claud Hamilton" 4–4–0s No. 62570 and 62612 in front of the shed and J15 0–6–0 No. 65460 beside the water column. *L.R. Peters*

An unusual, and possibly unique view of the interior of Wells engine shed on 29th June 1936. Class E4 2–4–0 No. 7422 stands on the short "loco siding" while, to the left, the "goods siding" passes *through* the engine shed to reach the goods shed at the rear. *H.C. Casserley*

The platform indicator at Wells-next-the-Sea in 1959. *H.B. Priestley*

The narrow gauge locomotive *Pilgrim* pauses in the loop at Walsingham prior to returning to Wells. Note the relatively large size of the train, which gives ample room for passengers and train crews. *Neville Fields*

Pilgrim is turned on the turntable at Walsingham, Lt-Com. Roy Francis can be seen in the cab. *Roy Francis*

Pilgrim at Wells in a view taken shortly after the opening of the Wells to Walsingham Railway. *Roy Francis*

tiple units into the area and effectively revolutionised services on the Wells branch and on the Dereham to Kings Lynn line. The revised, diesel-worked timetable provided ten trains each way between Norwich and Wells and twelve in each direction between Kings Lynn and Dereham. Some of the latter services ran through from Dereham to Norwich, while at other times good connections were available at Dereham. The new trains were popular with travellers who liked their companionable "open plan" interiors and novel "all round" windows (which gave people travelling in the front saloons a superb forward view of the line ahead). Although trains still stopped at all stations, the rapid acceleration after each intermediate stop enabled overall times to be cut to an average of about 90 minutes for the 43½ mile journey between Norwich and Wells.

Evidence of the improvements resulting from the introduction of modern rolling stock is provided by an examination of the June 1956 timetable. The day's train service began with the departure of the first down working which left Dereham at 6.04 am and arrived in Wells at 6.47 am. The flexibility of multiple unit operation allowed a turn-round to take place in a matter of minutes, and at 6.55 am the first up working of the day set off for Norwich, arriving in the county town by 8.34 am and allowing sufficient time for office workers to be at their desks by 9.00 am. Meanwhile, a second dmu had left Norwich at 6.35 am and, having passed the first up train at County School, it reached Wells at 8.03 am. A similar pattern of services was maintained throughout the day, with further return trips from Wells at 8.08, 9.49, 11.02 am, 12.10, 1.44, 3.15, 5.24, 7.18 and 8.18 pm. In all, there were ten up services between Wells and Norwich, balanced by nine down workings between Norwich and Wells and one short distance service between Dereham and Wells.

The apparently unbalanced distribution of up and down services was a result of the closure of Wells engine shed, which meant that stock was stationed overnight at Dereham; the short distance trips from Dereham to Wells were balanced by various other workings from Norwich or Kings Lynn.

By 1958, when the dieselisation of Norfolk branch services had been extended to other local lines, Dereham had become a stabling point for six dmu sets which jointly worked a complex series of diagrams covering services to Wells, Hunstanton, Ely, Thetford, Norwich and Kings Lynn.

It is perhaps worth pointing out that "dieselisation" was not necessarily synonymous with rationalisation of facilities, and the Wells branch did not become the kind of run-down "basic railway" associated with the later, post-Beeching era. Indeed, apart from the closure of Wells engine shed and the shortening of one or two platforms at intermediate stations, the branch retained most of its Victorian features; it remained fully signalled with (mainly) GER semaphores, and its expensive, fully-manned level crossings remained *in situ*. Freight traffic was still an important feature of branch operation, and the profitable full load, private siding traffic which emanated from Ryburgh mill and other rail-connected installations was the kind of bulk traffic that BR hoped to encourage in the years ahead.

In retrospect, there was still, by the 1960s, every reason to hope that the Wells branch would continue as a permanent part of BR's freight and passenger network. Wells was at last beginning to develop as a popular holiday centre, with a large caravan park and other facilities concentrated near the beaches to the north of the town. With the decline of commercial traffic in and out of Wells harbour the port was growing in favour as a yacht haven – while nearby Walsingham continued to attract growing numbers of pilgrims and Summer visitors.

Another encouraging sign was the growth in population at Fakenham, Dereham and Wymondham. The three towns had, for many years remained relatively small, with populations ranging from about 3,000 at Fakenham to over 5,000 at East Dereham and Wymondham. These figures increased significantly in the years following World War II, when Wymondham and Dereham virtually doubled in size. With freight traffic, particularly to Ryburgh (where the mill had been rebuilt following wartime damage) running at a healthy level, the Wells branch appeared to be one of East Anglia's more profitable rural branch lines.

Rundown and Closure

Sadly, the 1960s were the "Beeching Era", and at a time when the government of the day was making no secret of its dislike for nationalised industries, the publication of a report entitled *The Reshaping of British Railways* presaged doom for huge chunks of the BR network. Basing his findings on an extremely narrow financial model, Beeching concluded that rural lines carrying less than 17,000 passengers a week were "uneconomic" in cases where there was no other traffic. When freight traffic absorbed a proportion of the cost, the minimum acceptable passenger figure came down to 10,000 a week. The report took little cognisance of future population trends, but worse than this it seemed to apply its tests of viability in a highly selective way, taking sections of line in isolation from the main system and ignoring the fact that otherwise "unprofitable" branches might feed useful traffic onto main lines.

Inevitably, the Wells branch came under scrutiny and the northern extremity of the line was marked down for closure, leaving however a full passenger service between Norwich, Dereham and Kings Lynn. Freight traffic would continue as far as Fakenham, but the Wells to Dereham passenger service would be replaced by buses. The closure took effect from Monday 5th October, 1964, and the last trains ran on Saturday 3rd October; Wells retained its goods services for a further month, but by 31st October the line had closed for good beyond Fakenham. Goods facilities had, meanwhile, been withdrawn from Kimberley Park, Thuxton, Yaxham, County School and Walsingham.

On the face of it north Norfolk had escaped the worst of the Beeching axe, and the election of a new, less anti-railway government in 1964 seemed to guarantee the survival of lines that had escaped the initial pruning. The railway trade unions were confident that no Labour government would implement a large-scale closure programme, but in retrospect the new Labour administration was not as sympathetic as some commentators had predicted, and in 1968 Barbara Castle's Transport Act (which allowed socially-necessary routes to be subsidised by local authorities) did little to help *rural* lines. Plans published at the time showed a "basic system" of about 11,000 route miles, but on closure scrutiny, this revised railway network excluded many lines that had escaped the 1963 closure programme, and in Norfolk the basic system did not include the Lynn–Hunstanton, Lynn–Norwich, and Norwich–Sheringham lines. In effect, the "Castle Plan" had sentenced the southern end of the Wells line to death (unless of course local councils wished to provide some form of grant aid).

In the meantime the Norwich–Dereham–Kings Lynn route had not prospered and, faced with the prospect of a slow bus journey to Dereham station, most travellers from Wells or Fakenham to Norwich went direct to their destination by bus or private car, thereby depriving the Dereham–Norwich line of valuable through traffic. All stations became unstaffed halts in August 1966, but these economies did little to restore profitability, and the Dereham to Kings Lynn line was closed to passenger traffic on Saturday 7th September, 1968; the last day was marked by the running of an M&GN Society "East Anglian Branch Line Farewell" special.

Elimination of this further section of line contributed to a further reduction of through traffic on the surviving 11¼ miles of line between Wymondham and Dereham, and although the basic costs of the line were surely covered by its freight revenues, BR claimed that this last remnant of the Wells branch was still unprofitable, and proposed to axe the remaining dmu services.

The Wymondham to Dereham line was by this time merely a shadow of its former self; once the busiest section of the Wells

–Wymondham branch, it had been reduced to a single line branch with rationalised passenger facilities. At Yaxham, for example, all loops and sidings had been lifted and trains used the former down platform; the level crossing gates were manually-operated from an outside frame. At Dereham passenger trains terminated in the former down platform, and the down main line was severed just short of the level crossing. On the other hand, with significant quantities of freight traffic still being handled at Ryburgh, Dereham, Fakenham and North Elmham, the line retained much of its trackwork and signalling. Services, in these last months were handled by several multiple unit types, including Metro-Cammell, Cravens, and Gloucester RC&W sets. Branch freight services were usually hauled by class 31 A1A-A1As.

On 15th September, 1968 the doomed line was involved in another flood drama, comparable to that of 1912. It had rained more or less continuously for several days,and the rain persisted for a full 24 hours on 14th–15th September, creating chaos in the Norwich area. Norwich itself was cut off by earth slips on the Ely, Ipswich and Yarmouth lines, and until these lines could be brought back into service the only available permanent way materials were on the recently-singled Wymondham to Dereham branch. Two engineer's trains were therefore sent onto the branch to recover ballast and other materials for use on the damaged main lines, and branch passenger services were temporarily suspended while these operations took place.

Although still relatively popular with local travellers, the Dereham branch finally lost its passenger services on Saturday 4th October, 1969. There have nevertheless been persistent efforts to secure a restoration of dmu services between Wymondham and Fakenham, and this locally-based campaign was intensified after the 1974 oil crisis increased the cost of private motoring.

In 1975 the "Wymondham, Dereham & Fakenham Railway Action Committee" was formed as a result of a meeting called by the East Anglian Branch of the Railway Invigoration Society, and these two related organisations have, for several years, been campaigning for a reinstatement of passenger services. Pointing out that the line remains in being as a freight route, the campaigners argue that some form of railbus or dmu service could be provided at very little cost. On 8th April, 1978, local action committees organised a special train from Norwich to Dereham, and over 600 people took the opportunity to travel on the otherwise freight-only branch. The six-car multiple unit formation made two return trips, attracting considerable attention in Dereham and at intermediate stations such as Yaxham and Hardingham. A similar dmu special was run by the Railway Development Society on 28th September, 1985.

FAKENHAM.

PARKER'S SIDING BETWEEN FAKENHAM AND WALSINGHAM.

Wagons to and from this siding must only be worked by Up trains.

WELLS.

INWARDS FREIGHT TRAINS.

On arrival of a Freight train from either the West Norfolk, Norwich, or Harbour lines, and it is found that the train is too long for the engine to run round and lower the wagons into the station, the operation of dropping the wagons down under the control of the hand brake must only be carried out under the personal supervision of the Foreman Porter or man in charge, who must see that all is clear, and the points set for the road into which the wagons are required to run.

ASSISTING WEST NORFOLK BRANCH PASSENGER TRAINS OUT OF STATION.

Whenever absolutely necessary, an engine may assist a West Norfolk Branch Passenger train out of Wells Station towards Holkham by pushing it in the rear, but the assistant engine must always be accompanied by the Station Master or Foreman Porter. The Signalman must also be advised as to what is about to be done before the train is allowed to leave.

The operation must be carried out with great care, and in no case must the assistant engine go beyond the overline bridge, about 160 yards on the Holkham side of Wells Station Down Home signal, and, whenever possible, the Driver of the assistant engine must be in possession of the "Wells-on-Sea and Burnham Market" train staff.

The assisting of the train out of the station is purely a shunting operation, and the assistant engine is not to be block-signalled in any way.

The Signalman at Wells Station must, after the train and assistant engine have passed the West Norfolk Branch Up Starting signal, place and maintain that signal at danger, and place a lever collar on the lever working this signal. The lever collar must not be removed until the Signalman has been verbally informed by the Station Master or Foreman Porter that the assistant engine has returned and been passed clear of the West Norfolk Branch Single line.

County School—		
Station Box	To or from Fakenham and the Back Platform ...	4 short
	To or from Aylsham and the Main	3 short
	To or from Aylsham and the Back Platform ...	2 short
Dereham—		
Central Box	To or from King's Lynn line and Main Passenger Station	3 short
	To or from King's Lynn line and Back Platform line...	2 short, pause, 2 short
	To or from King's Lynn line and Goods Shed line ...	5 short
North Box	Main, to or from the Goods Shed line	2 short
West Junction Box	From the Siding North of the King's Lynn line to the Up King's Lynn line	3 short, pause, 3 short
Wells-on-Sea—		
Station Box	To or from Dereham line and West Norfolk line Platform	2 short
	To or from Dereham line and Sidings East of the Passenger Station	2 short, pause, 2 short
	To or from West Norfolk line and West Norfolk line Platform	3 short
	From Harbour line to Platform line	5 short

WYMONDHAM—WELLS-ON-SEA.

Wymondham and Dereham ...	Up and Down trains	60
Dereham and Wells-on-Sea ...	Up and Down trains	50
County School	Over Loop line	15
Fakenham Station	Up trains over Loop line	15
Wells-on-Sea	Trains from Fakenham when approaching Station	15

NOTE.—Until further notice no train must exceed a speed of 60 miles per hour.

Extracts from the General Working Appendix.

The BR Line Today

The withdrawal of regular passenger services allowed BR to implement further economies, and the line was soon reduced to a long siding, worked on the "one engine in steam" system; most level crossings were worked by train crews, resulting in extended journey times for the surviving freight workings. Public goods traffic was handled at North Elmham and Ryburgh until July 1971, the two stations remaining open thereafter for private siding traffic. Coal class traffic was still accepted at both Dereham and Fakenham, but the main sources of bulk freight are now grain and fertiliser. There has, in recent years been just one freight working each way daily, taking up to five hours for the 23½ mile journey between Wymondham and Ryburgh.

Continuing rationalisation has obviously reduced facilities, though much of interest remains. At Wymondham the junction has been remodelled and the branch is now entered via a single turnout from the down main – trains from Norwich must reverse onto the down line before continuing northwards onto the branch.

From Wymondham the BR route continues as a single line to Dereham, where facilities are surprisingly complex; the former goods shed is trackless although much of the track layout remains *in situ* to serve adjacent maltings and granaries. The station buildings continue to serve the public as a bus depot. Similarly, at North Elmham a loop and sidings have been retained to serve R.J. Seamen & Sons' grain silos, while at Ryburgh the extensive private sidings remain intact.

The future of the section northwards to Fakenham is at present in some doubt, though at the time of writing the line still handles occasional fertiliser traffic. The two storey station buildings at Fakenham are occupied by BR and the National Bus Company and have remained in good repair. Elsewhere on the line, station buildings at Kimberley Park, Hardingham, Thuxton, Yaxham and County School are occupied as private dwellings and remain intact.

Eventual Re-opening?

If re-opened, the Wymondham to Fakenham line could provide useful public transport facilities for the growing towns of Dereham (pop. now 10,000), Wymondham (pop. 10,000) and Fakenham (pop. 4,500). One problem might be the large number of level crossings which would require modest investment if they were to be replaced by automatic lifting barriers; the need to accommodate freight traffic in addition to railcar-worked passenger services would also require investment in some form of new signalling. In spite of these potential problems, the case for reinstatement would seem to be sound –

though much would depend on the attitude of local authorities *vis-à-vis* the question of grant aid. North of Fakenham, re-opening would be much harder to justify, but happily there has already been a reinstatement of the line between Wells and Walsingham, where (as we shall see) an extremely interesting narrow gauge railway is now flourishing on the former trackbed. When the Wells & Walsingham line is extended southwards to Fakenham, the entire branch will once again be back in use – albeit with a break of gauge!

Looking ahead, it may not be too fanciful to envisage through journeys being made between Norwich and Wells-next-the-Sea, with a change from nationally-owned diesel trains to privately-run steam trains at Fakenham. The resulting transport facilities would probably not attract many "serious" travellers through to Wells, but in an age of growing leisure the presence of a steam-worked narrow gauge railway at Fakenham would do much to enhance the future prospects of any revived BR service between Norwich, Dereham and Fakenham.

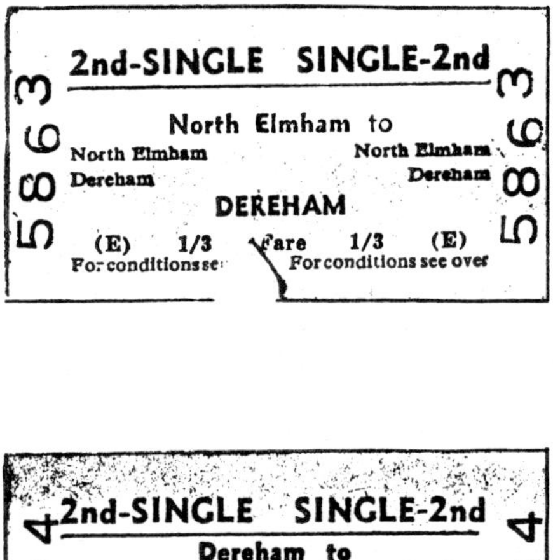

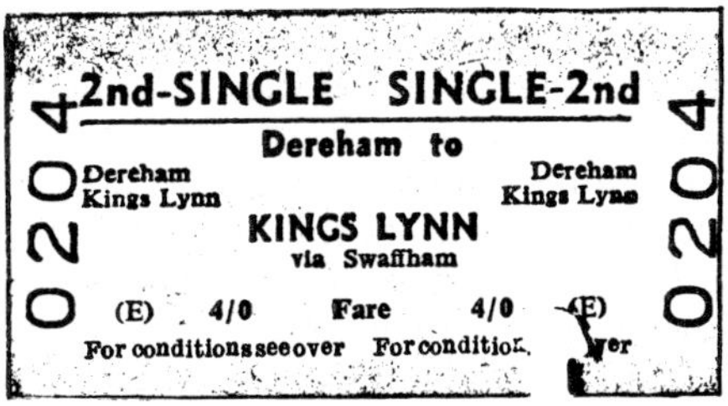

Chapter Seven

Revival at Wells: The Wells & Walsingham Railway

The abandoned Fakenham to Wells section of the branch was dismantled after the cessation of freight services, but the former trackbed remained substantially intact throughout its 9½ mile length. At Wells, the redundant terminal buildings eventually found a new lease of life as a pottery, while (even more unusually) Walsingham station was adapted for use as a place of worship by the Russian Orthodox Church.

In the meantime, Wells had blossomed as a holiday resort in its own right, attracting considerable numbers of caravaners, boating enthusiasts and other self-catering holidaymakers. Aware that the area had potential for further development, the newly-created North Norfolk District Council actively promoted the little town, advertising it (along with the established resorts of Mundesley, Cromer and Sheringham) in guides prepared mainly for tourists and holidaymakers. With the quays cleared of railway lines, the Wells "waterfront" at last began to look like a real promenade, and with its quaint old streets and houses, Wells-next-the-Sea could stand comparison with any other seaside town.

First Steps

In 1975 the District Council asked Lieutenant-Commander Roy Francis, a retired naval officer, to build a miniature railway between Wells harbour and the beaches and caravan parks at "Abraham's Bosom"; this would provide a further attraction for holidaymakers while at the same time fulfilling a need for transport between Wells and its beaches. The result was the mile-long Wells Harbour Railway, a 10¼ in. gauge miniature railway which provided a timetable service at 40 minute intervals throughout the Summer.

The harbour line was highly successful, but once it was complete and in operation, Lt-Com. Francis felt that there would be scope for a much longer 10¼ in gauge line which would allow this unusually-narrow gauge to be exploited to its full potential as a *means of transport*. Driving past the abandoned Wells branch every evening, he realised that the formation – which connected the holiday centres of Wells and Walsingham – was sufficiently intact to provide a foundation for his projected narrow gauge line. Of equal significance was the thought that people staying in Wells (or touring the area by car) would welcome the chance to travel to Walsingham by steam railway and there would thus be a market for the new railway. Although the purchase of 4 miles of disused railway would be an immensely costly

STATUTORY INSTRUMENTS

1982 No. 521

TRANSPORT

The Wells and Walsingham Railway Light Railway Order 1982

Made - - - - -	*5th April* 1982
Coming into operation	*6th April* 1982

The Secretary of State for Transport on the application of Lt. Commander Roy Wallace Francis R.N. Rtd. and Marie Eleanor Francis and in exercise of powers conferred by sections 7, 9, 10 and 11 of the Light Railways Act 1896(**a**), as amended by the Light Railways Act 1912(**b**) and Part V of the Railways Act 1921(**c**), and section 121(2) of the Transport Act 1968(**d**) and now vested in him(**e**) and of all other powers enabling him in that behalf hereby makes the following Order:—

Citation and commencement

1. This Order may be cited as the Wells and Walsingham Railway Light Railway Order 1982 and shall come into operation on 6th April 1982.

Interpretation

2. In this Order, unless the context otherwise requires, the following expressions have the meanings hereby respectively assigned to them:—

"the Board" means the British Railways Board;

"the Board's railway" means the railway or former railway of the Board described in Schedule 1 to this Order;

"the level crossing" means the level crossing at Warham St. Mary;

"the proprietors" means Lt. Commander Roy Wallace Francis R.N. Rtd. and Marie Eleanor Francis,

"the proprietors' railway" means the railway authorised to be constructed, made and maintained by the proprietors pursuant to article 5 of this Order;

"the Secretary of State" means the Secretary of State for Transport;

"the principal Act" means the Light Railways Acts 1896 and 1912, as amended by the Railways Act 1921.

Light Railway Order for the Wells and Walsingham Light Railway.

exercise, further research suggested that the project was viable, and once committed, Lt-Com. Francis soon put his scheme into effect, acquiring the necessary land and obtaining a light railway order for the proposed line.

Once these obstacles were overcome, the rest was, in a sense, easy, and construction proceeded with commendable speed. Most of the heavy works were already in existence, but there was a major problem at the place known locally as "Barnard's Cutting", where thousands of tons of refuse had been tipped by the local council. Around 3,000 tons were removed, but in the end it was decided to lay the rails *over* the remaining infil – the result being a gradient which would test the miniature locomotives to their limit!

Unlike many other light and narrow gauge lines, the "Wells & Walsingham" railway was designed and built as an efficient means of transport, using as many modern ideas and materials as possible – the object being to run the line cheaply and efficiently with the minimum of staff and no unnecessary frills. The choice of gauge was an important aspect of Lt-Com. Francis's scheme for, although much narrower than usual, it could be maintained by a two-man permanent way crew without the need for cranes or other heavy lift equipment. Much of the line was laid with channel or "U"-shaped steel rail which had already proved itself in operation on the Wells Harbour line. At stations, conventional 20 lb per yard flat-bottomed rail was employed, this being more convenient for the construction of pointwork.

Narrow Gauge Locomotives and Rolling Stock

The design of locomotives and rolling stock was another important aspect of the railway and, as with the trackwork, Lt-Com. Francis incorporated many innovations in his initial locomotive and passenger vehicles. The first locomotive was built by D.H. King of Suffield, Norfolk in 1981/2, and displaying considerable historical prescience, the Lt-Com. decided to call it *Pilgrim*. The new locomotive was an 0–6–0T with 4 in. x 6 in. outside cylinders and a boiler diameter of 14 in. Suspension was achieved by a combination of springs on the centre axle and hard rubber blocks on the leading and trailing axles; total weight, in working order, was one ton. Despite its small dimensions, *Pilgrim* was a narrow gauge rather than a miniature locomotive – in other words it was a full size engine running on 10¼ in. gauge track; the cab for instance was designed to accommodate a fully grown man in reasonable comfort. All bearing surfaces were fabricated from standard parts, with generous surfaces to ensure free running. Externally, the engine was finished in a mid green livery, with polished brass boiler bands, dome, whistle and safety valves.

WELLS WALSINGHAM RAILWAY

• NOW • OPEN •

The longest 10¼" gauge railway in GREAT BRITAIN

A timetable service from the seaside and harbour town of **WELLS** to the picturesque town of **WALSINGHAM** famed for centuries as a centre of pilgrimage. A scenic journey with *five bridges* through lovely countryside. Halts at **WARHAM St. MARY** and **WIGHTON.**

THE RAILWAY IS OPEN 7 DAYS A WEEK FROM EASTER TO SEPTEMBER 30th.
EASTER WEEK: TABLE 1, THEN TABLE 2 UNTIL SPRING BANK HOLIDAY.
SPRING BANK HOLIDAY TO MID-SEPTEMBER: TABLE 1.
MID-SEPTEMBER TO SEPTEMBER 30th: TABLE 2.

TIMETABLE 1.

WELLS DEPART	WALSINGHAM DEPART
10.00 a.m.	10.40 a.m.
11.20 a.m.	12.00 noon
12.40 p.m.	1.20 p.m.
2.00 p.m.	2.40 p.m.
3.20 p.m.	4.00 p.m.
4.40 p.m.	5.20 p.m.

Please arrive early for your train particularly during peak periods (i.e. mid-morning and mid-afternoon).

TIMETABLE 2.

WELLS DEPART	WALSINGHAM DEPART
10.30 a.m.	11.15 a.m.
12.00 noon	12.45 p.m.
2.00 p.m.	2.45 p.m.
3.30 p.m.	4.15 p.m.

JOURNEY TIME: 25 minutes in each direction.

There is plenty of time to look around Wells or Walsingham before catching a later train home.

Rolling stock at the time of opening consisted of an air-braked, articulated set, running on rubber block suspension and seating 38 passengers. Special refinements included a wheel-driven compressor to ensure a supply of air for the main braking system, and electric bell communication between guard and driver. Designed to run as an integral unit with *Pilgrim*, the coach at the Wells end of the train had a built-in water tank to supplement the engine's small capacity side tanks. An electric compressor ensured an additional source of air, and there were also two hand pumps; the whole braking system was twin-line and failsafe, with emergency valves in the covered guard's compartments at each end of the articulated set.

Some Features of the Line

The Wells & Walsingham Railway was opened for the carriage of passengers on 6th April, 1982, from which date a basic train service of six trains each way has again connected Wells, Walsingham and Wighton Halt; an additional stopping place was established at Warham St Mary. Journey time, for the four mile journey, is 25 minutes in each direction. At Wells, the new railway starts and terminates near the former A149 level crossing, where facilities originally consisted of a simple run-round loop, with a turntable and a short dead-end siding.

From Wells, the line continues southwards along the trackbed of the Wells & Fakenham Railway, with excellent views of the sand dunes, nature reserve and sea, together with many tantalising glimpses of picturesque Norfolk villages and churches. The steady climb up to Barnard's Cutting ensures that locomotives must work flat out to lift their 6 ton trains over the summit, and lineside photographers and recording enthusiasts are rewarded with the unique sights and sounds of a steam locomotive achieving an optimum performance under everyday conditions. At Walsingham, the line terminates in a leafy cutting, a short distance to the north of the original station. Facilities here include another turntable and run-round loop.

The line, which is worked as efficiently as possible on the "one engine in steam" system, has no need for expensive signalling installations, but under the terms of its Light Railway Order the Wells & Walsingham is responsible for the provision of fixed warning boards at Warham St Mary Level Crossing, and these must be illuminated whenever the railway is used during the hours of darkness.

The Wells & Walsingham is primarily a passenger line, but in common with other railways it needs a small number of "goods" vehicles for permanent way work and the carriage of locomotive coal, and there are at present two such vehicles on the line – both transferred from the original Wells Harbour line. One of these service wagons is a large bogie coal vehicle, while the other is a Hudson tipper wagon which has been regauged from 2 ft to 10¼ in.

As with PW vehicles, there has been some inter-change of locomotives between the W&W and Wells Harbour lines, and in the interests of completeness these "visitors" should be mentioned. As *Pilgrim* was not delivered until 1982, the W&W line was built with the aid of *Weasel* – an 0–4–0 petrol engined shunter built by D.H. King of Suffield, which with its full size cab and green livery looks very much like an internal combustion engined version of *Pilgrim.* A later acquisition was an unnamed 0–6–0 petrol-mechanical engine, which was built by Alan Keef Ltd of Cote, near Bampton (Oxfordshire) in 1985; this locomotive, with its fully-roofed central cab, is a typical "industrial" shunter. A complete list of locomotives and rolling stock used on the W&W at the time of writing is given in **Table 5** (*below*).

Table 5

WELLS & WALSINGHAM LOCOMOTIVES & ROLLING STOCK (AS AT 12/1985)

LOCOMOTIVES

Weasel	0–4–0	petrol-engined shunter, built by D.H. King of Suffield.
Pilgrim	0–6–0T	steam locomotive, built by D.H. King of Suffield, 1981.
—	0–6–0	petrol-engined shunter built by Alan Keef of Bampton, 1985.

ROLLING STOCK

5-vehicle articulated set with covered guard's compartments.
1 open bogie freight wagon, used mainly for coal.
1 former 2 ft gauge tipper wagon transferred from Harbour line.

Liveries at the time of opening were dark green for locomotives and red for rolling stock. Boiler bands, domes, and other details are kept highly-polished, recalling those far-off Edwardian days when Great Eastern 2–4–0s ran along the single track branch to Wells-next-the-Sea. The line, by its very nature, lacks sophisticated lineside buildings, and it is perhaps a pity that (apart from bridges) so little of the former standard gauge infrastructure could be used. There are nevertheless one or two minor structures, including a wooden engine shed and lineside hut at Wells, together with a miniature water tank supported on a stack of unused sleepers.

Towards the Future

Future plans include the opening of a 4-mile extension from Walsingham to Fakenham, and when brought to fruition this will give the Wells & Walsingham Railway an overall length of 8¾ miles (it is already the longest 10¼ in. gauge line in the world). There are also plans for a fully-enclosed, steam-heated rake of coaches and – of even greater interest – *Norfolk Hero,* a large Beyer-Garratt 2–6–0+0–6–2 locomotive which was built in 1986. Over 20 ft long, *Norfolk Hero* must be the most powerful 10¼ in. gauge engine in the world, with a generously-proportioned boiler suspended between two powered bogies. Benefiting from the lessons learned with *Pilgrim,* the new locomotive has roller bearings, a large footplate and cab, and ample provision for coal and water fuel.

When completed throughout to Fakenham, the present day Wells & Walsingham Railway will have succeeded in reviving almost all of the former Wells & Fakenham route, and it would be fitting to conclude with the thought that the W&F – built so long ago – has found a new lease of life in the last quarter of the 20th Century; one feels that Hall Keary, Joseph Southgate, Richard Till, and the other Victorian pioneers would be proud to know that their branch has survived so long.

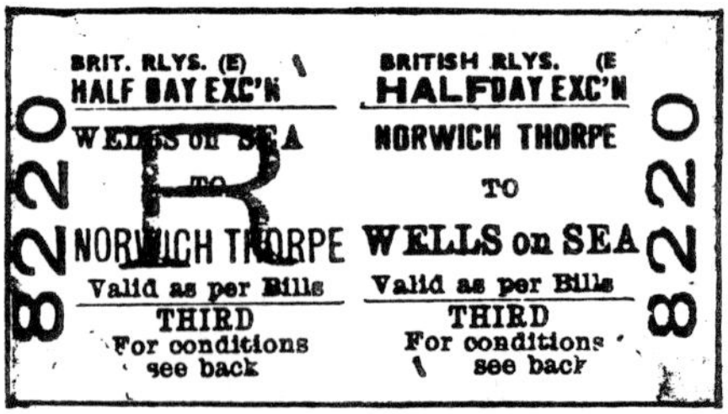

Bibliography

Valuable insights into the early history of the Norfolk Railway, the Wells & Fakenham Railway, and the West Norfolk Railway were obtained from contemporary editions of the *Railway Times* – which frequently printed Director's reports verbatim for the benefit of potential investors. This material was supplemented by annual reports and financial statements appearing in *Bradshaw's Shareholders' Manual* – which also yielded useful information on Boardroom changes throughout the 19th Century. Information on individual Directors was culled from the *Dictionary of National Biography,* (or in certain cases from gravestones and church monuments). Other sources for the early periods included the *Railway Magazine,* the *Great Eastern Railway Magazine,* and the *Locomotive Magazine.* For more recent periods, GER, LNER and BR public and working timetables gave details of train services, distances and working arrangements, while topographical information was obtained from a variety of sources including Ordnance Survey Maps, *Kelly's Directories* and RAF navigational charts. Personal recollections were also of immense help, and the author would like to extend special thanks to Roy Francis. Help with photographs and other illustrations came from Lens of Sutton, Edwin Wilmshurst, G.R. Mortimer, Colin Judge, Canon Charles Bayes, Alan Taylor and H.C. Casserley.

The following books and articles were consulted, and although many are long out of print, all contain extra details for those seeking further details of Norfolk railways, or Norfolk local history in general.

Cecil J. Allen, *The Great Eastern Railway* (1955)

E.L. Ahrons, The Locomotives of the GER, *Locomotive Magazine* Vols 7–18, 1901–1912

David J. Bosher, Norfolk Postscript, *Railway Magazine* Vol. 126, February 1980.

Michael Crofts, Minimum Gauge to Walsingham, *Railway Magazine* Vol. 129, June 1983

N. Crump, *By Rail to Victory* (1947)

W.A. Dutt, *The Little Guide to Norfolk* (1902)

W.R. Jenkinson, The Predecessors of the Great Eastern Railway, *The Great Eastern Magazine* 1913–15

R.S. Joby, *Forgotten Railways of East Anglia* (1977)

Donald I. Gordon, The Lynn & Dereham Railway, *Railway Magazine* Vol. 102, 1958

Donald I. Gordon, *A Regional History of the Railways of Great Britain* Vol. 5 (1968)

J.F. Gairns, The Norfolk Lines of the LNER, *Railway Magazine* 1929

A.W. Purchas, *Some History of Wells-next-the-Sea* (1965)

G.W. Potter, The Great Eastern Railway in West Norfolk, *Railway Magazine* 1910

H.H. Meik, The East Anglian Railway, *Railway Magazine*

R. Murman, Plan of the Month: Wells-next-the-Sea, *Railway Modeller* Vol. 32 April 1981

Rly Invogoration Society, *Can Bus Replace Train* (1977)

Alan Summers, Maunsel Parva to Wells, *Railway Modeller* Vol. 24 February 1973

E. Tuddenham, A Journey to Wells-next-the-Sea, *Railway World* Vol. 26 March 1965

Appendix One

Promoters, Directors and other Prominent Personalities

Thomas Coke, Earl of Leicester (1752–1842): The celebrated "Coke of Norfolk", who inherited Holkham in 1776 and transformed the hitherto barren estate into an agricultural show piece.

Thomas William Coke, Earl of Leicester (1822–1909): Succeeded his father in 1842 and continued improving the estate; generally acknowledged as the "founder" of the Wells & Fakenham Railway but it is conceivable that the whole project was initiated by local traders who, out of deference, would have taken their scheme to the Earl at an early date. T.W. Coke was nevertheless a major subscriber and without his support the line would not have been built; he took little obvious interest in the day to day operation of the line, but was probably well-briefed by Hall Keary.

Sir Samuel Morton Peto (1809–1889): Born in Woking, Surrey, Peto made his fortune as a railway contractor, in which capacity he was no doubt a brilliant organiser and a good employer; he always (for example) gave considerable thought to the spiritual welfare of rough, otherwise lawless navvies, and local historians have identified clear links between the progress of his railways and the spread of Baptist chapels. Unfortunately Peto tended to exert a strong "political" influence on companies with which he was involved, and these influences grew as Peto's own wealth and prestige increased. Perhaps unintentionally, he was directly responsible for the Wells & Fakenham's problems *vis-à-vis* the Eastern Counties Railway, and having created this problem he seems to have made little attempt to rescue the smaller company. Peto was associated with numerous lines, including the Norfolk, East Suffolk, Oxford Worcester & Wolverhampton, South Eastern, London Tilbury & Southend, Eastern Counties, and Metropolitan District Railways. Peto usually worked in conjunction with Edward Ladd Betts, trading as Mesrs Peto & Betts; the firm went bankrupt following the failure of bankers Overend & Gurney in 1866, and Peto never recovered his lost prestige.

Hall William Keary: A Wells & Fakenham Director, and apparently one of its most committed supporters; he usually chaired public meetings of the company.

Joseph Southgate: A coal and corn dealer of Wells, and like Hall Keary, one of the most committed W&F supporters; he may have been the first to suggest the scheme, but as a mere trader he would not have been able to act without the Earl of Leicester.

Richard Till: Chairman of the Norfolk Railway and a Director of the Wells & Fakenham – in which capacity he evidently felt himself at the centre of the W&F/ECR imbroglio, and tried his hardest to solve the problem.

George Berkeley: An experienced engineer, though much of his work was overseas on foreign or colonial lines such as the Marseilles Extension and Great Indian Peninsula Railways; the W&F was a very minor project in comparison, and Berkeley is unlikely to have spent much time in North Norfolk.

Horatio Love: Chairman of the ECR from 1856, and first Chairman of the GER, Love made only small concessions towards the Wells & Fakenham; he negotiated with Richard Till during the months before opening but would not honour the 46 per cent operating agreement arranged by Morton Peto.

Appendix Two

Signalboxes and Signalling

Signalbox	*Levers*	*Notes*
Wells-next-the-Sea	45	
Walsingham	19	
Parkers Siding	5	ground frame
Fakenham North	37	39 levers after 1928
Fakenham South	25	abolished 1928
Ryburgh	25	Saxby & Farmer frame
Broom Green	–	abolished 1880s
County School	44	Saxby & Farmer frame
North Elmham	20	
Dereham North	24	
Yaxham	26	
Thuxton	18	
Hardingham	21	abolished 1968
Kimberley	–	
Wymondham S. Jcn	42	

Note: Most Wells branch boxes had MacKenzie & Holland frames.

Dereham North and Hardingham signalboxes. *R. Humm Collection*

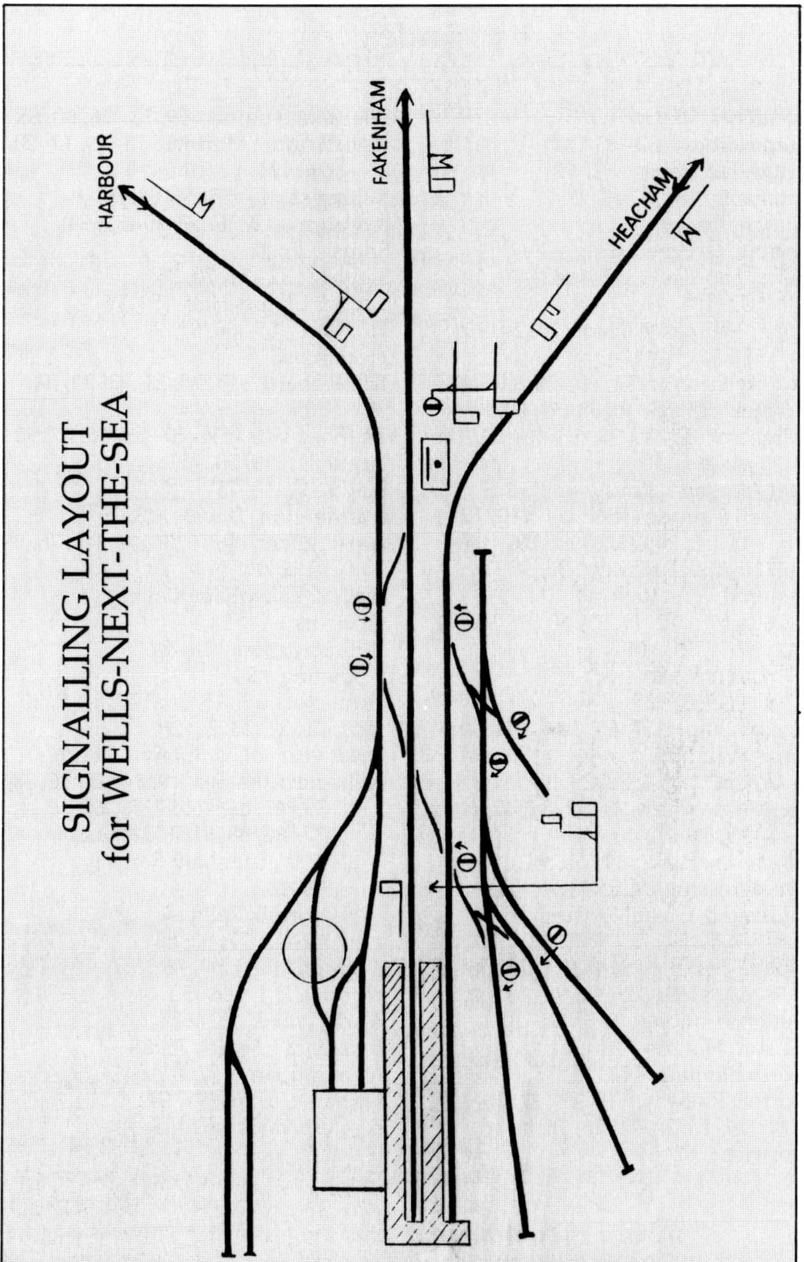
SIGNALLING LAYOUT
for WELLS-NEXT-THE-SEA
HARBOUR
FAKENHAM
HEACHAM

Index